Teach Learn Guide

A Resource Book for Home and School

Donna Moore McMillan

Vander Publishing House

Teach Learn Guide

A Resource Book for Home and School

Donna Moore McMillan

Vander Publishing House

Manufactured in the United States of America

Copyright © 2018

ISBN-13:978-0692945759(Vander Publishing House)

ISBN-10: 069294575X

All rigts reserved. No part of this publication may be reproduced, stored in a retrieval system, or transmitted, in any form or by any means, electronic, mechanical, photocopying, recording or otherwise , except as permitted under section 107 or 108 or the 1976 United States Copyright Act, without the prior written consent of the author or publisher.

Introduction

Teach Learn Guide is a resource tool designed to use in both the home and classroom setting. The format of the book is design to be simple enough for parents to teach basic handwriting, math, and reading skills. Educators will discover that the information provided is an excellent supplement for lesson plans. In addition, the creative activities included in the book, encourages student learning and participation.

Table of Contents

Back to Basic:	pg.7
Lines, Shapes and Colors...............	pg.8
Writing A to Z	pg.63
ABC'S..	pg.64
Handwriting Sheets.......................	pg.65
Writing 1-10.................................	pg.91
Math	pg.102
Equals10......................................	pg.103
Subtracting 10.............................	pg.109
Numbers 11-19............................	pg.121
Adding to 20...............................	pg.127
Basic Addition.............................	pg.132
Basic Subtraction........................	pg.136
Adding Two Digits.......................	pg.139
Subtracting Two Digits................	pg.141
Ten to One Hundred...................	pg.143
Back to School By Tens..............	pg.148
Big..	pg.161
Small..	pg.162
Tall...	pg.163
Long..	pg.164
Position.......................................	pg.165
Number Line................................	pg.167
Graphs..	pg.169
Fraction......................................	pg.172
Less/Greater Than.......................	pg.178
Place Value.................................	pg.179
Introduction to Money...............	pg.181
Health...	pg.197
Food..	pg.206
Science..	pg.213

Table of Contents

Time	pg.223
Months Days Year	pg.224
Telling Time	pg.228
Musical	pg.239
Transportation	pg.249
History:	pg.258
Pledge of Allegiance	pg.259
The Bald Eagle	pg.260
America the Beautiful	pg.261
These United States	pg.262
District of Columbia	pg.314
Continents and Oceans	pg.315
Reading Comprehension	pg.318
Sight Words	pg.319
Stories	pg.320
Literature:	pg.329
My Shadow	pg.330
Dreams	pg.331
Trees	pg.332
A Tisket –A Tasket	pg.333
Good Morning Song	pg.333
Twinkle Little Star	pg.334
Baa Baa Black Sheep	pg.334
Loop de Loop	pg.335
It's Raining	pg.335
Thumbelina	pg.336
The Tale Of Peter Rabbit	pg.339
The Princess and The Pea	pg.356
Four Seasons	pg.359
Just For Fun	pg.388
Acknowledgements	pg.401

Back to Basics

Follow the direction of the arrows using a red crayon

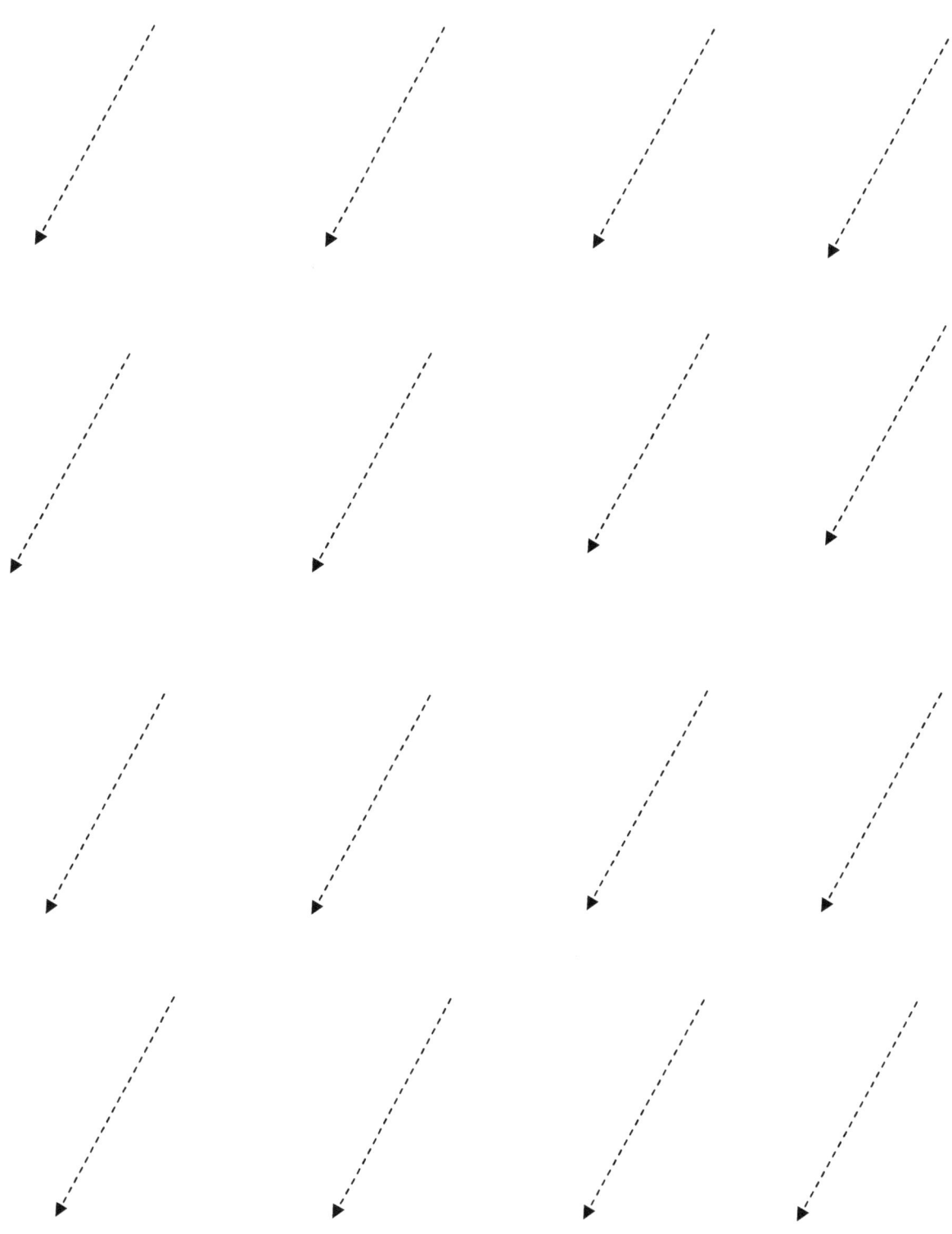

Trace the lines using a red crayon

Draw lines using a red crayon

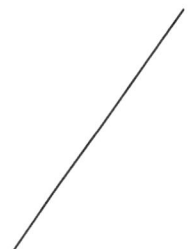

Follow the directions of the arrows using an orange crayon

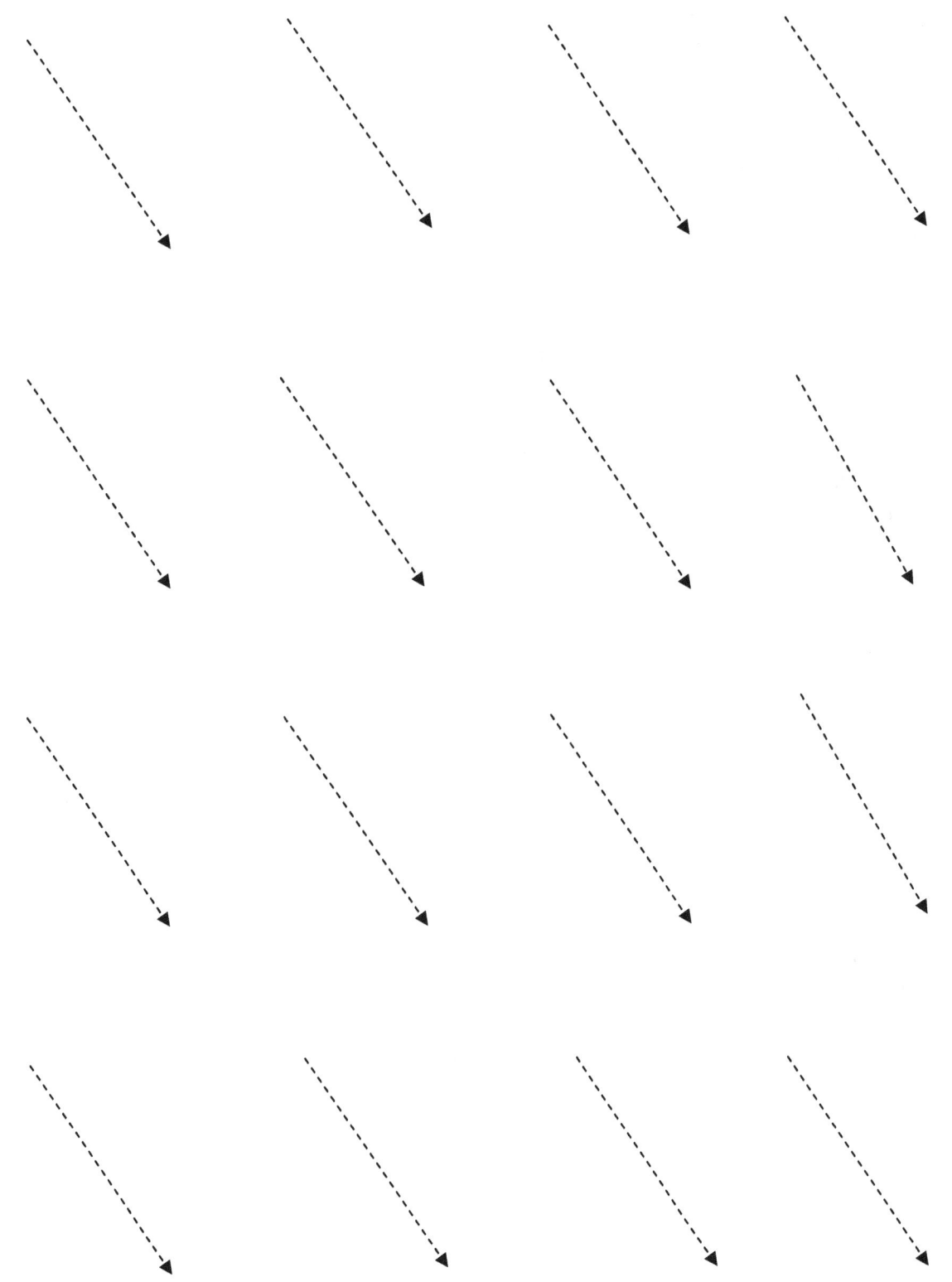

Trace the lines using an orange crayon

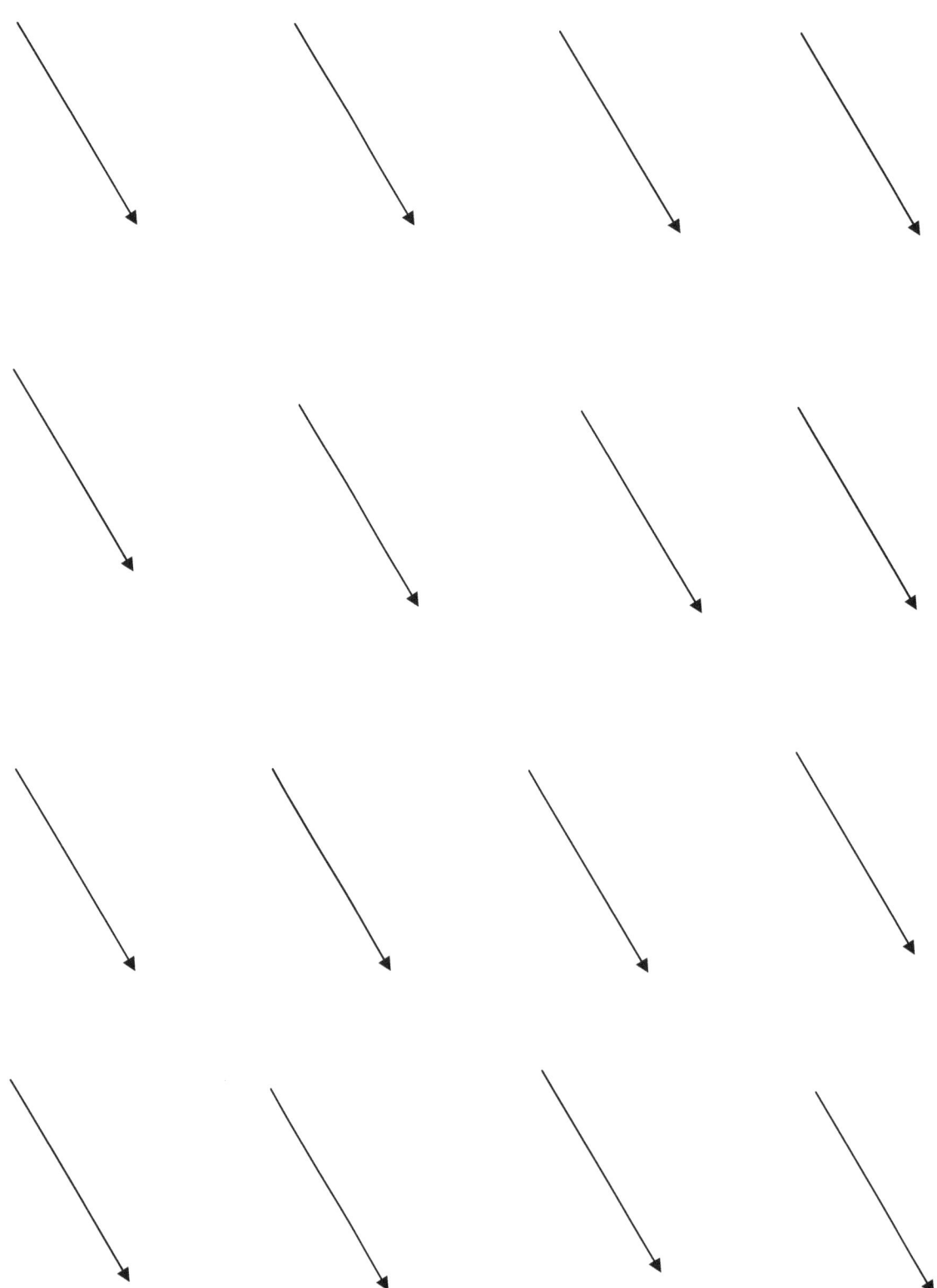

Draw lines using an orange crayon

Follow the directions of the arrows using a brown crayon

14

Trace the lines using a brown crayon

Draw lines using a brown crayon

———————

Review Time

Draw the lines

17

Drawing Triangles

Follow the direction of the arrows using a green crayon

Trace the lines using a green crayon

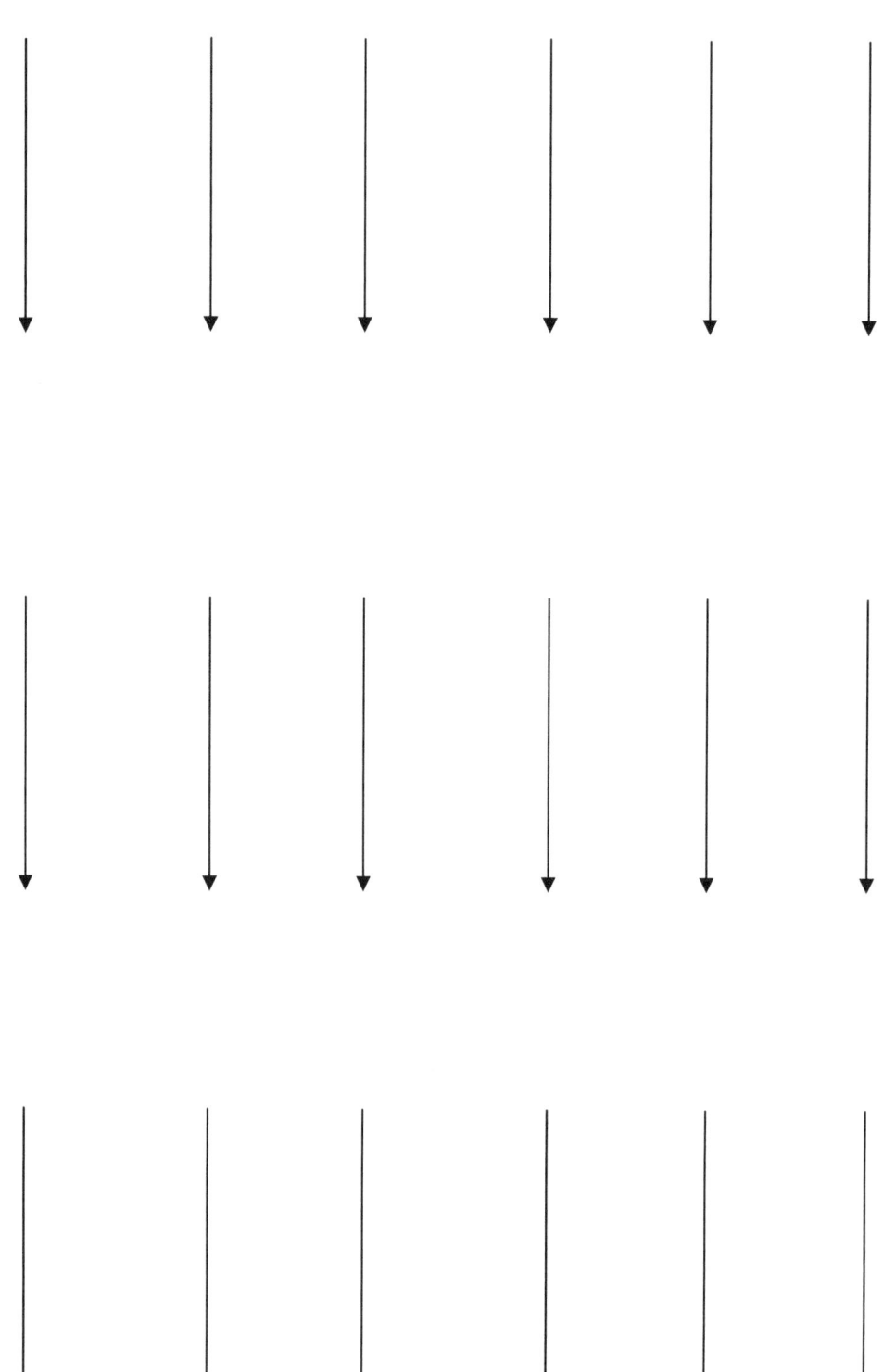

Draw lines using a green crayon

Drawing Squares

22

Drawing Rectangles

23

Review Time
Draw The Lines

Drawing Pentagons

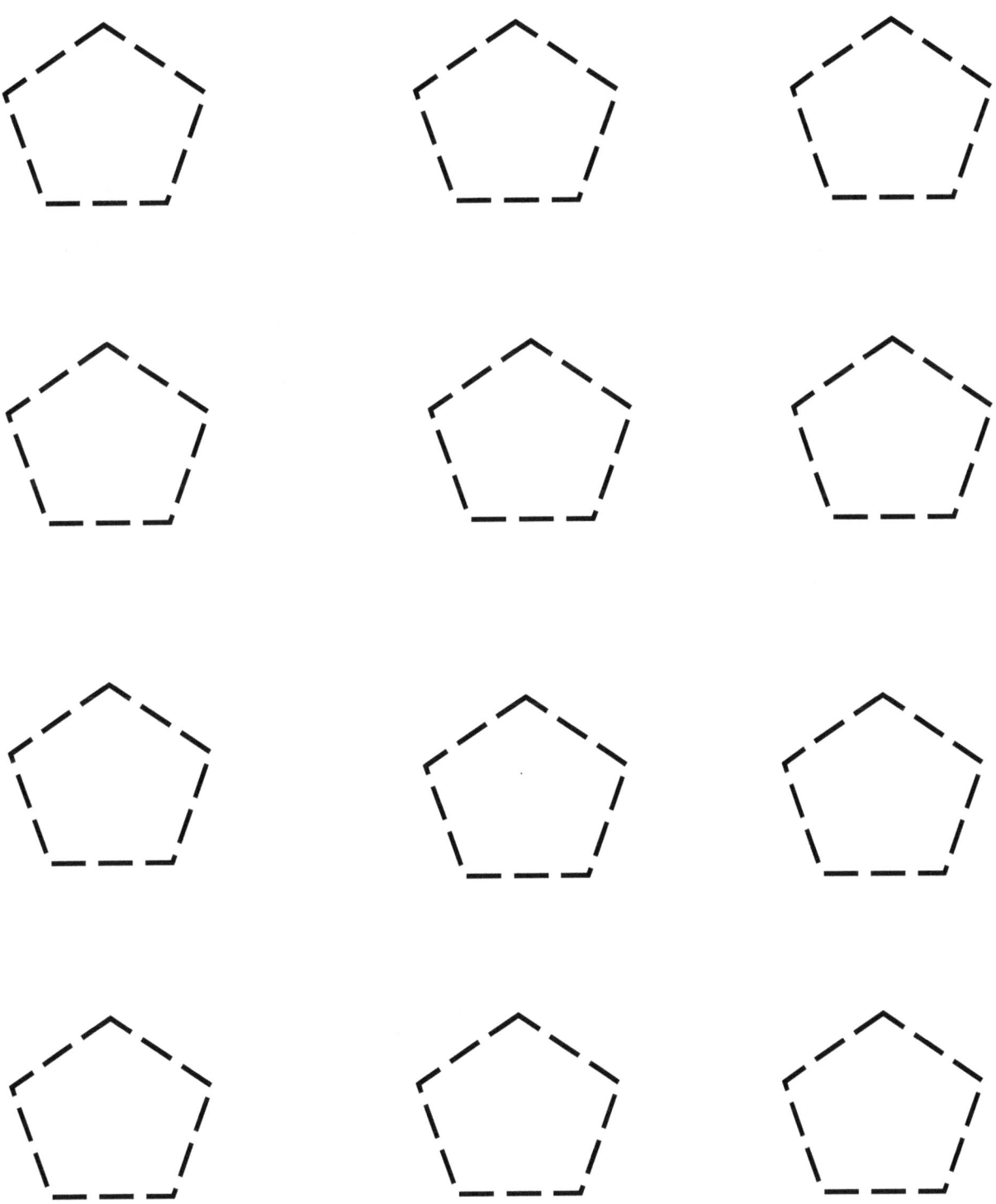

Follow the directions of the arrows using a yellow crayon

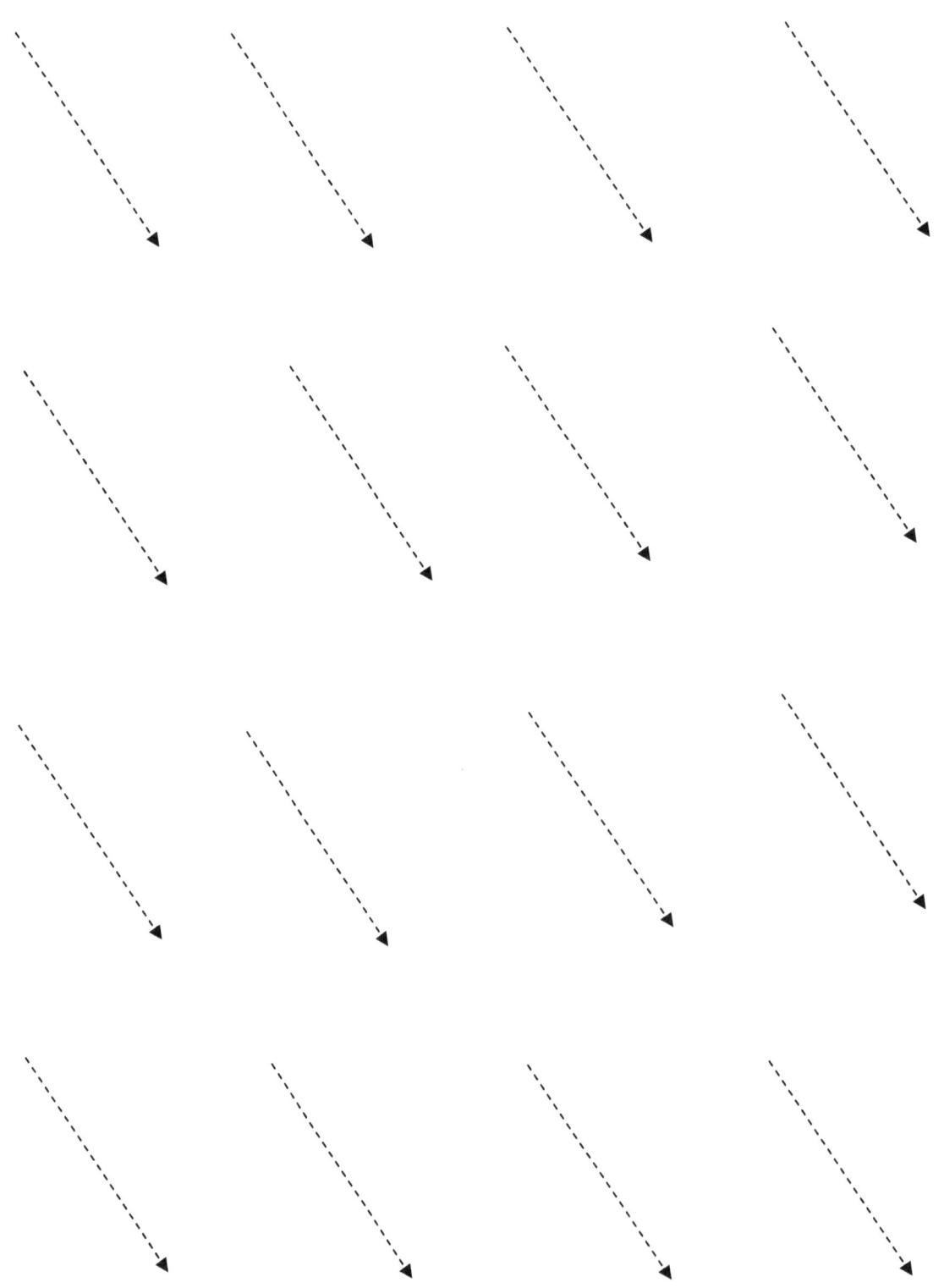

Trace the lines using a yellow crayon

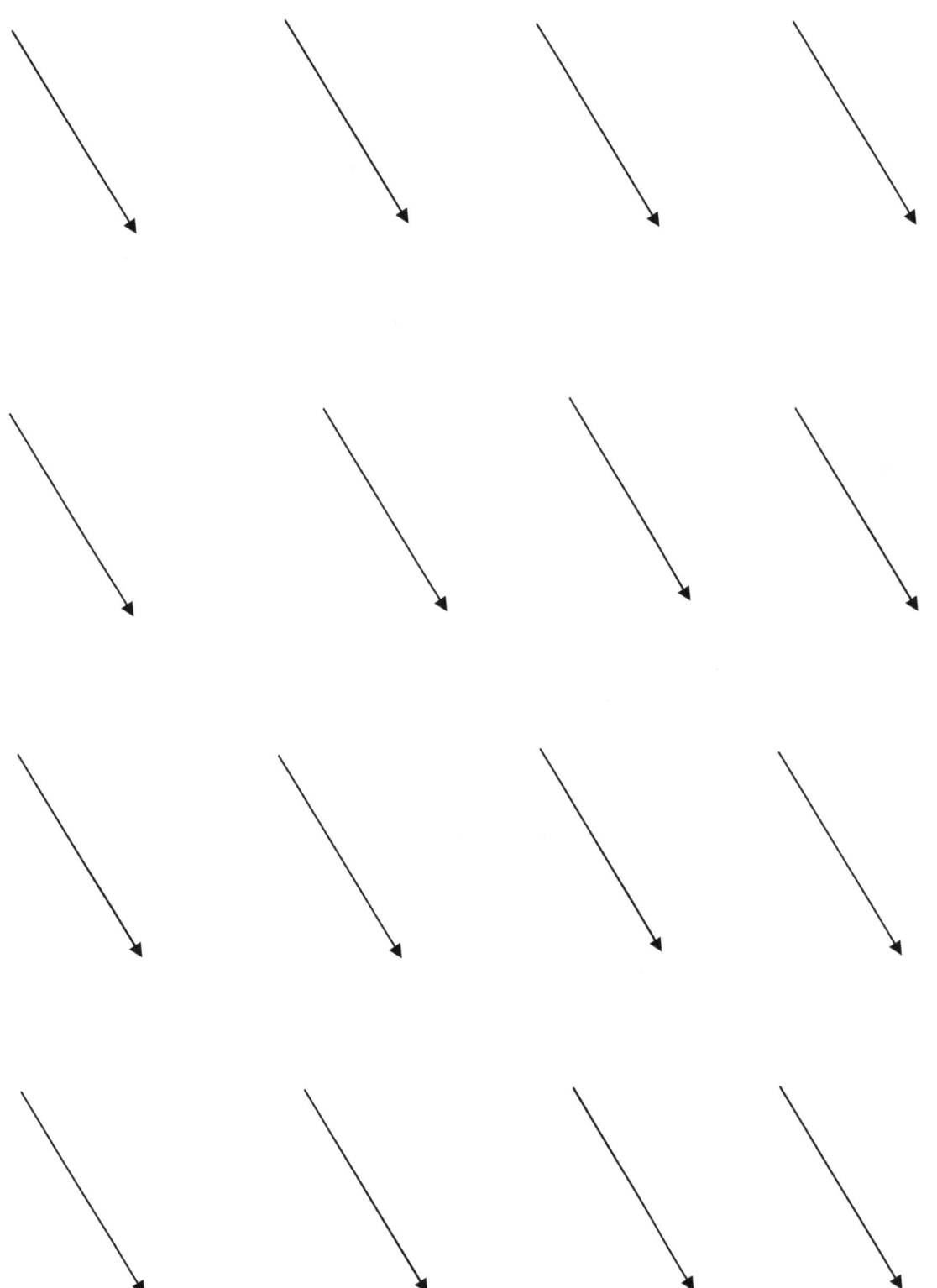

Draw lines using a yellow crayon

Follow the direction of the arrows using a blue crayon

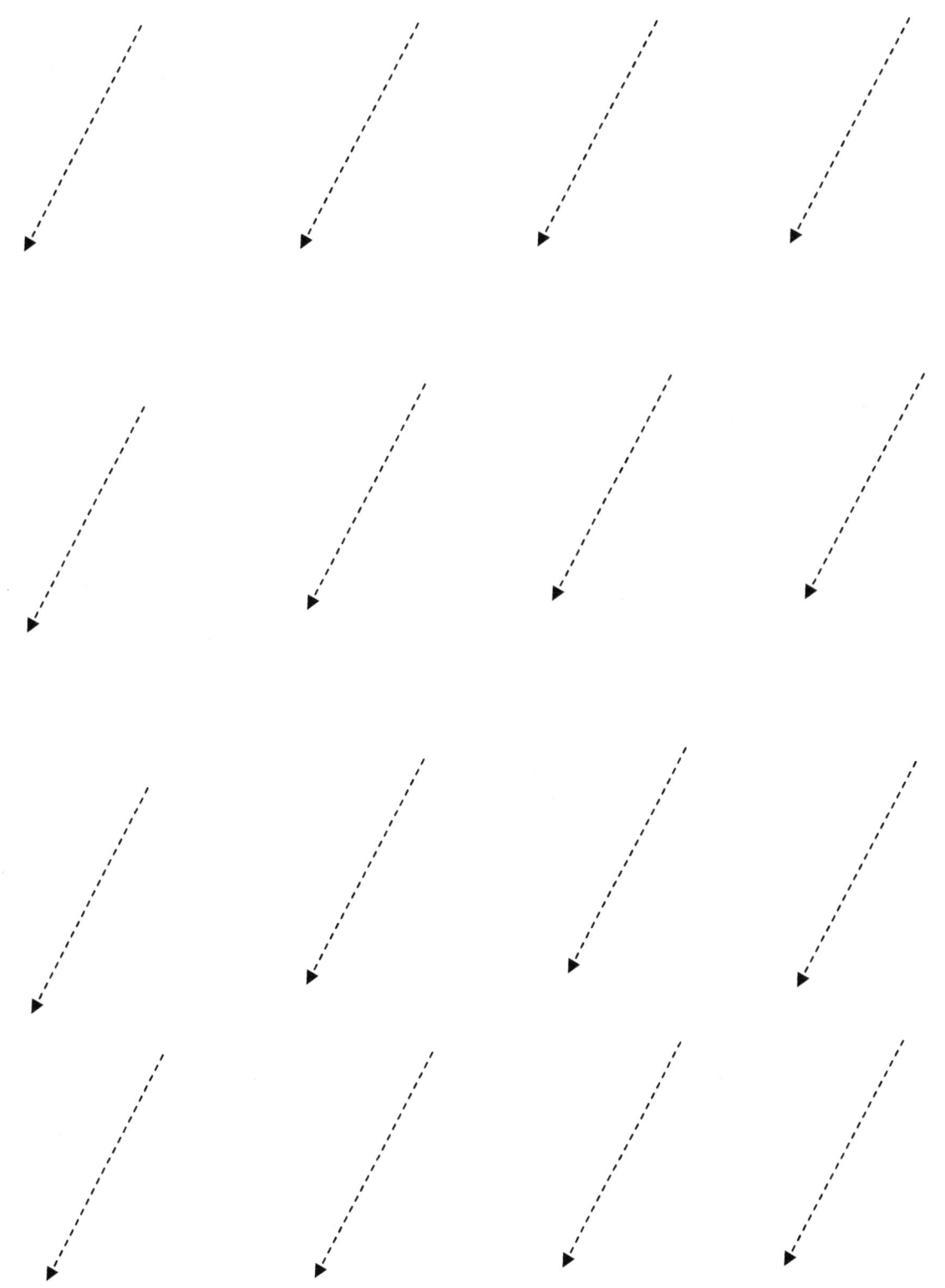

29

Trace the lines using a blue crayon

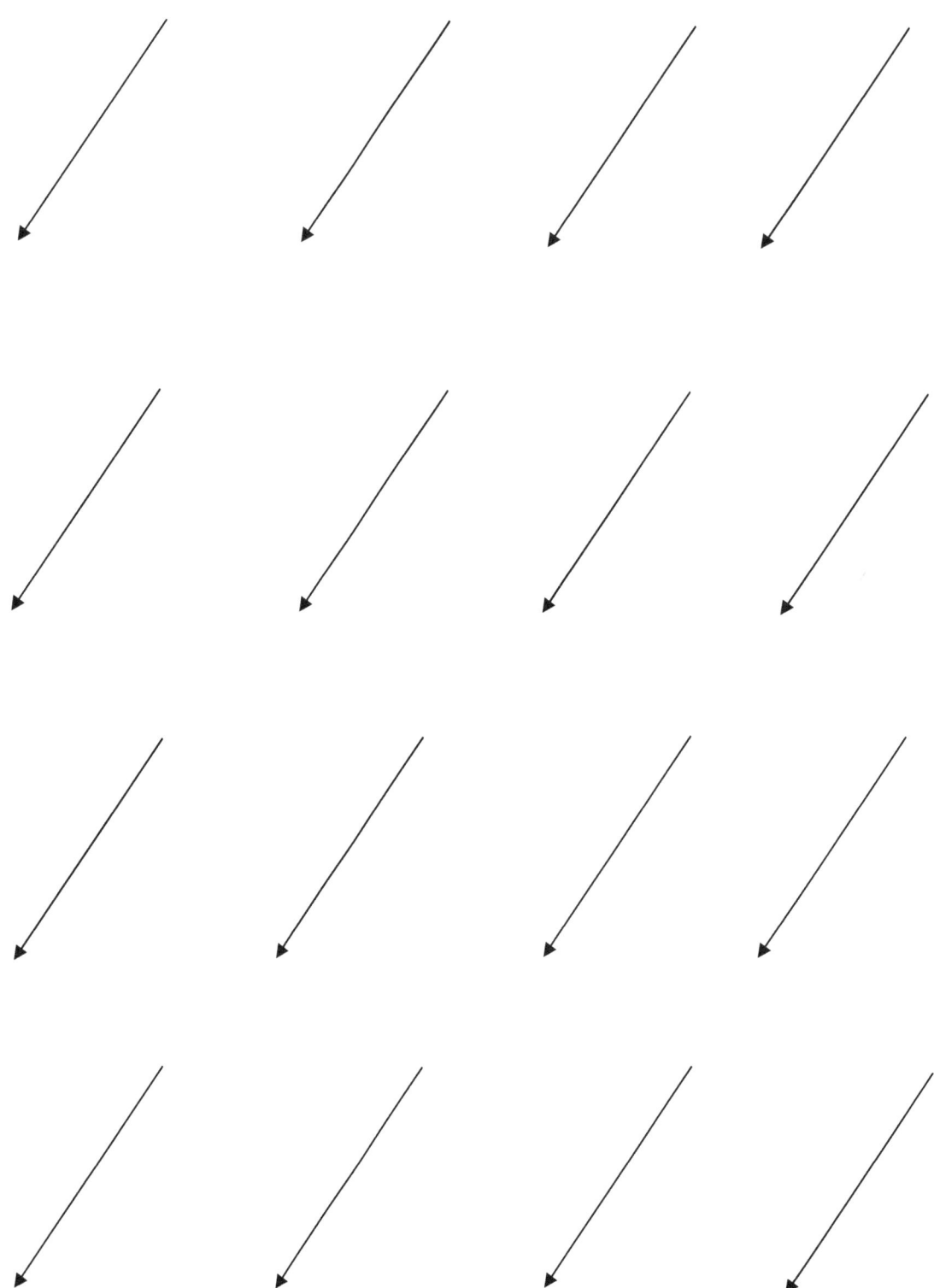

Draw lines using a blue crayon

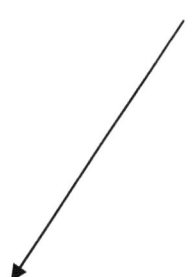

Drawing Diamonds (Parallelograms)

Review Time

Draw each of the lines in a different color

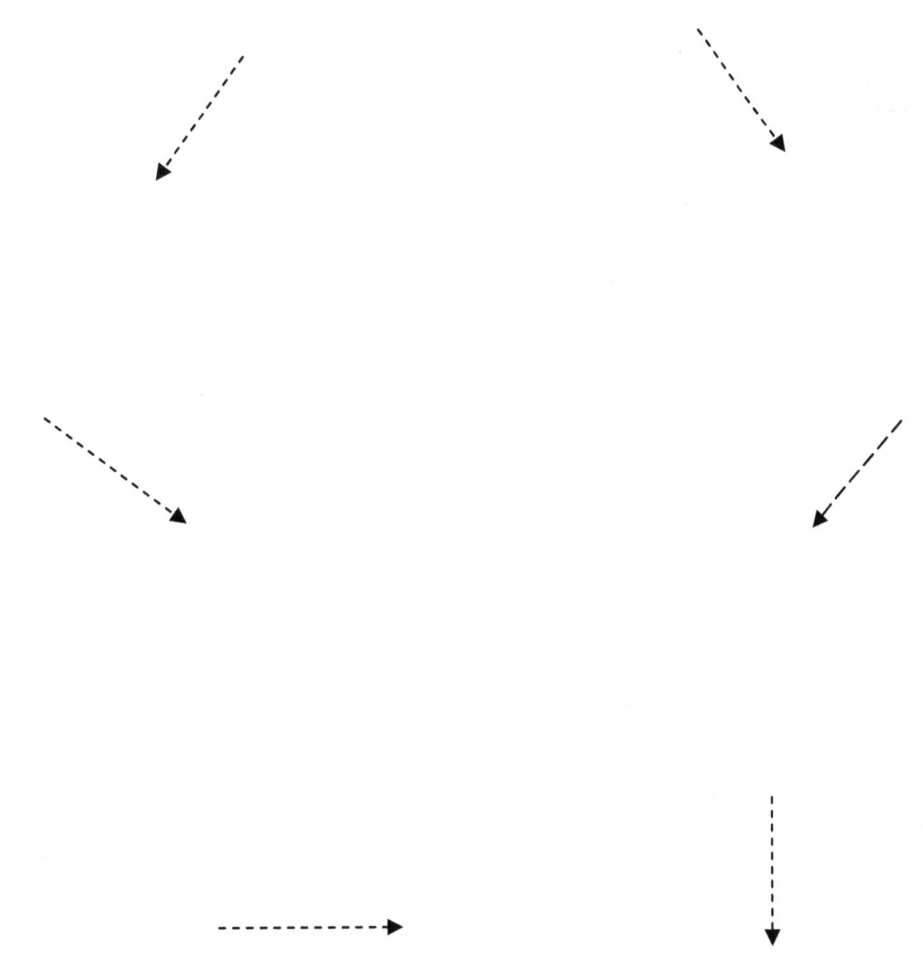

Drawing Hexagons

Review Time

Draw each shape

Color each shape using a different color

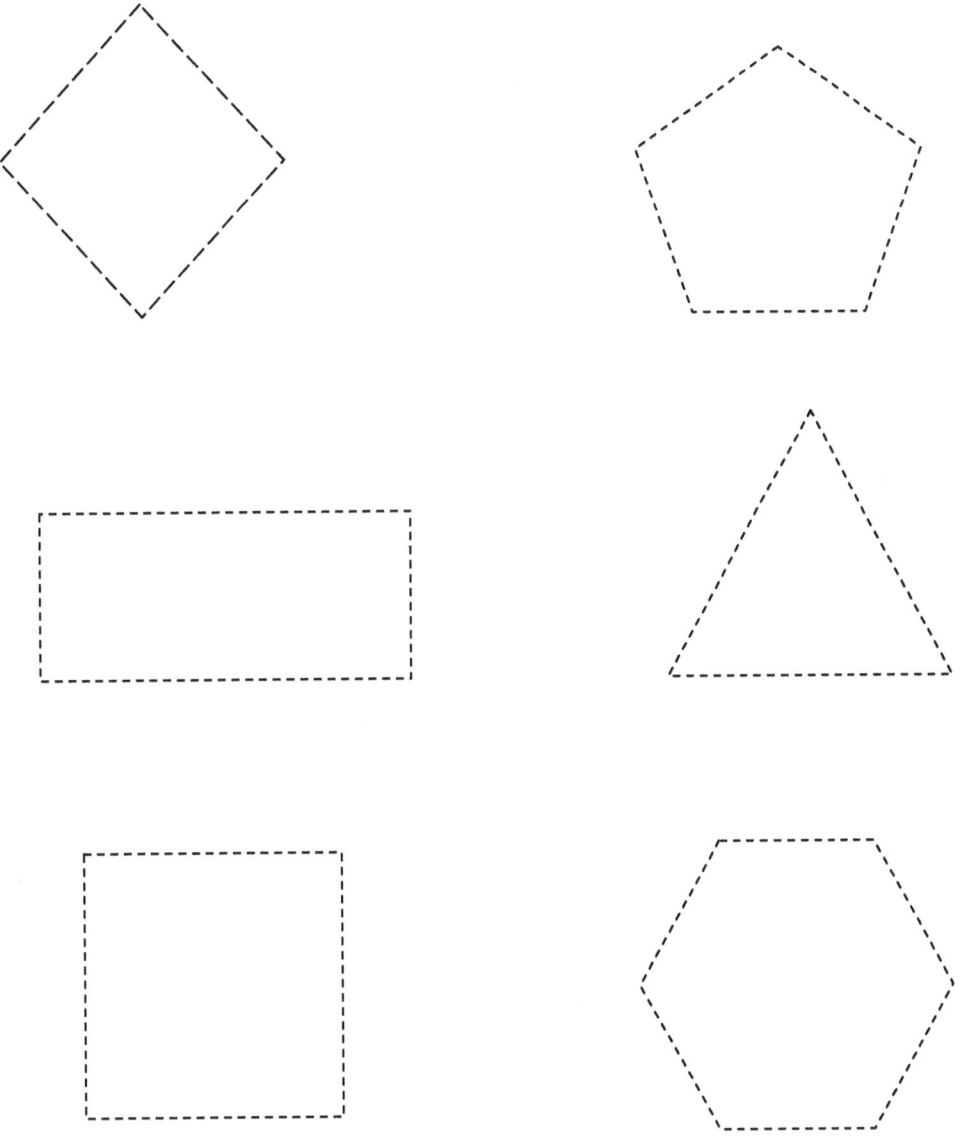

Follow the direction of the arrows using a purple crayon

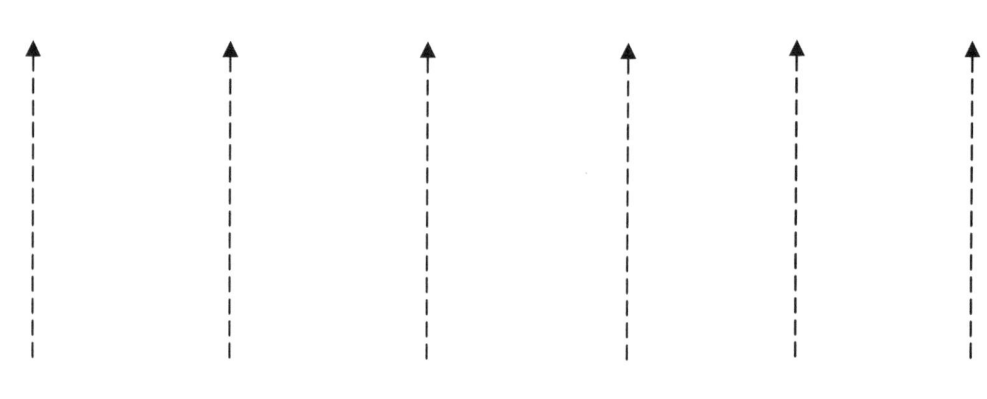

Trace the lines using a purple crayon

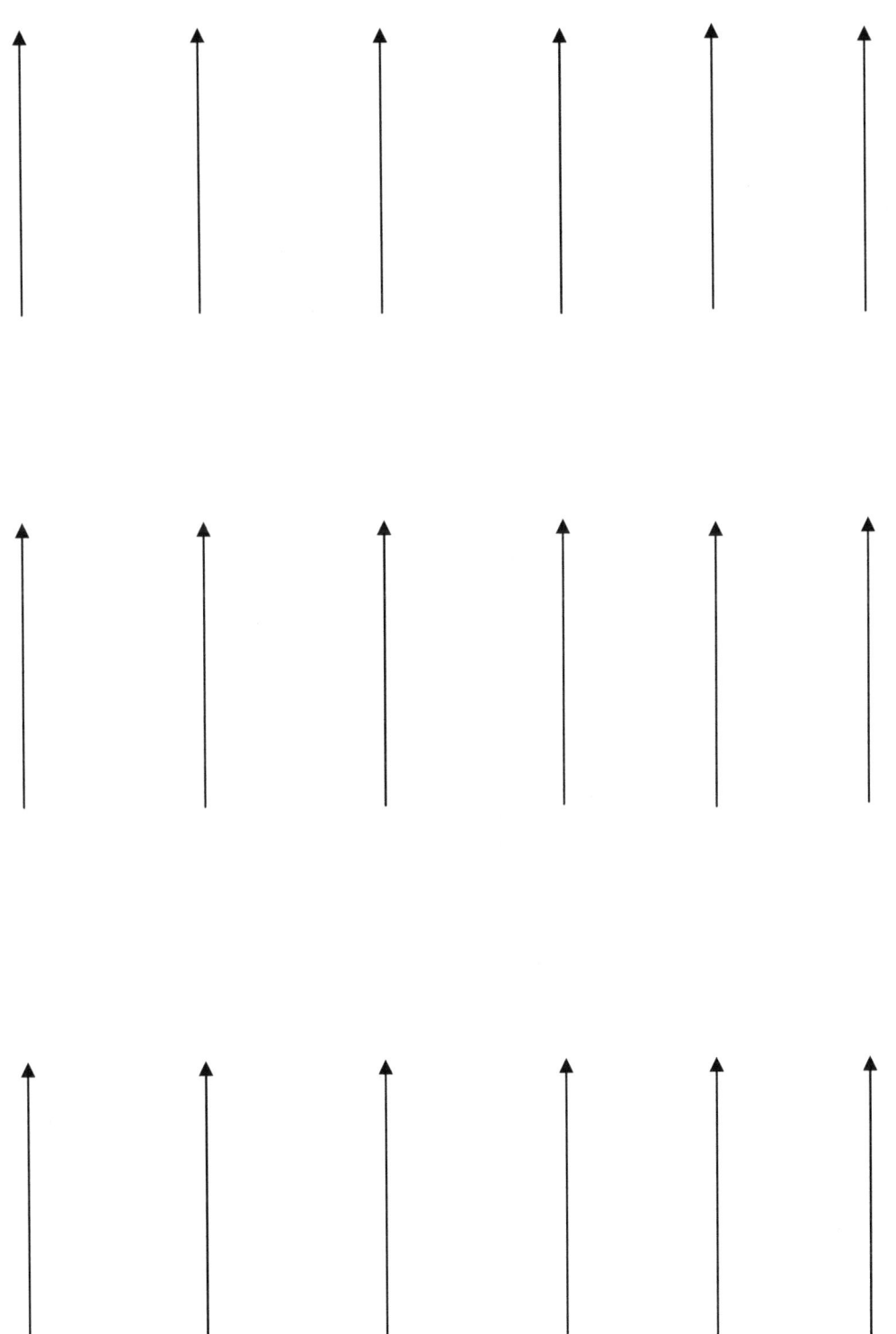

Draw lines using a purple crayon

Drawing Octagons

Follow the directions of the arrows using a black crayon

Trace the lines using a black crayon

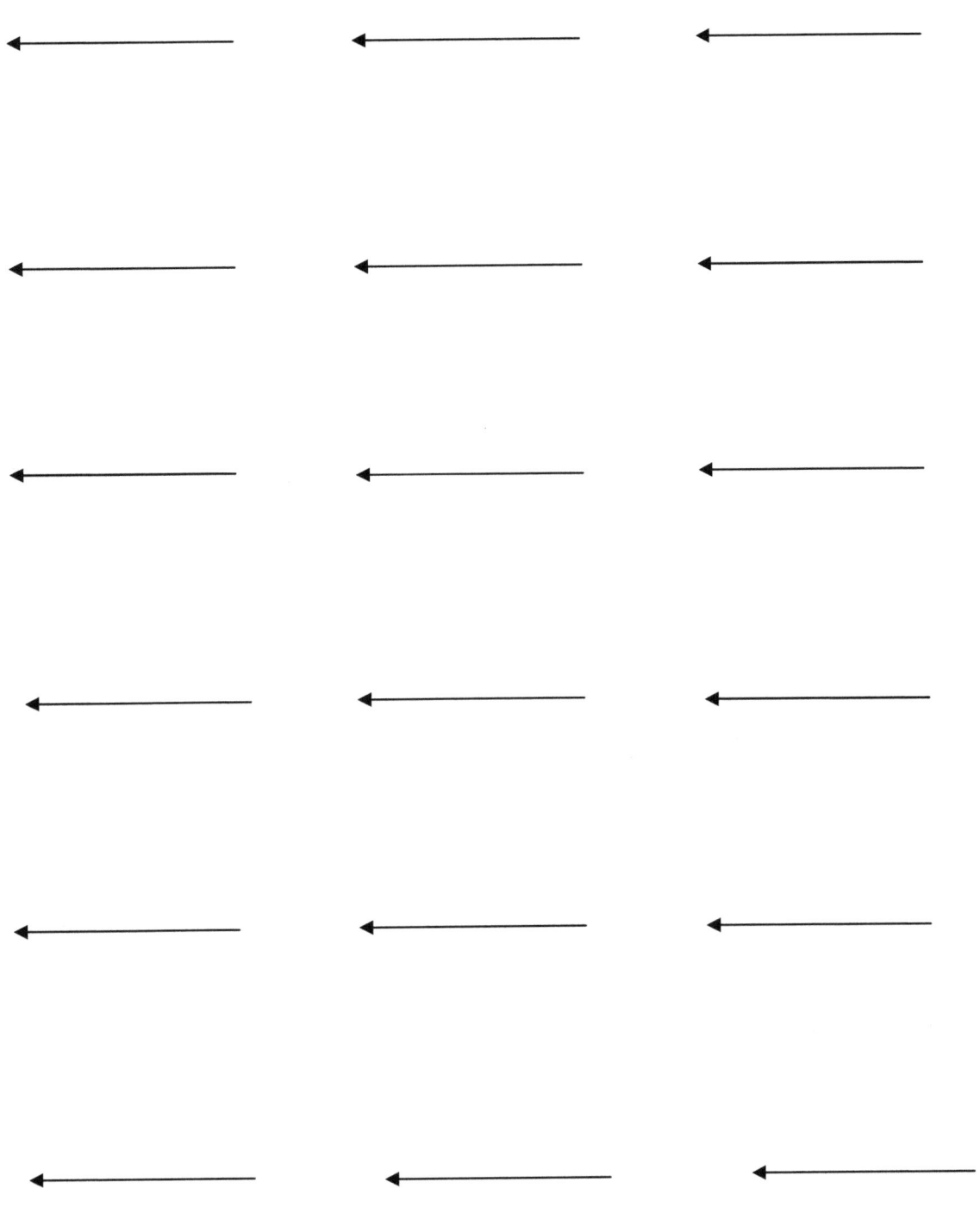

Draw lines using a black crayon

———————

Drawing Stars

43

Reviewing All Lines

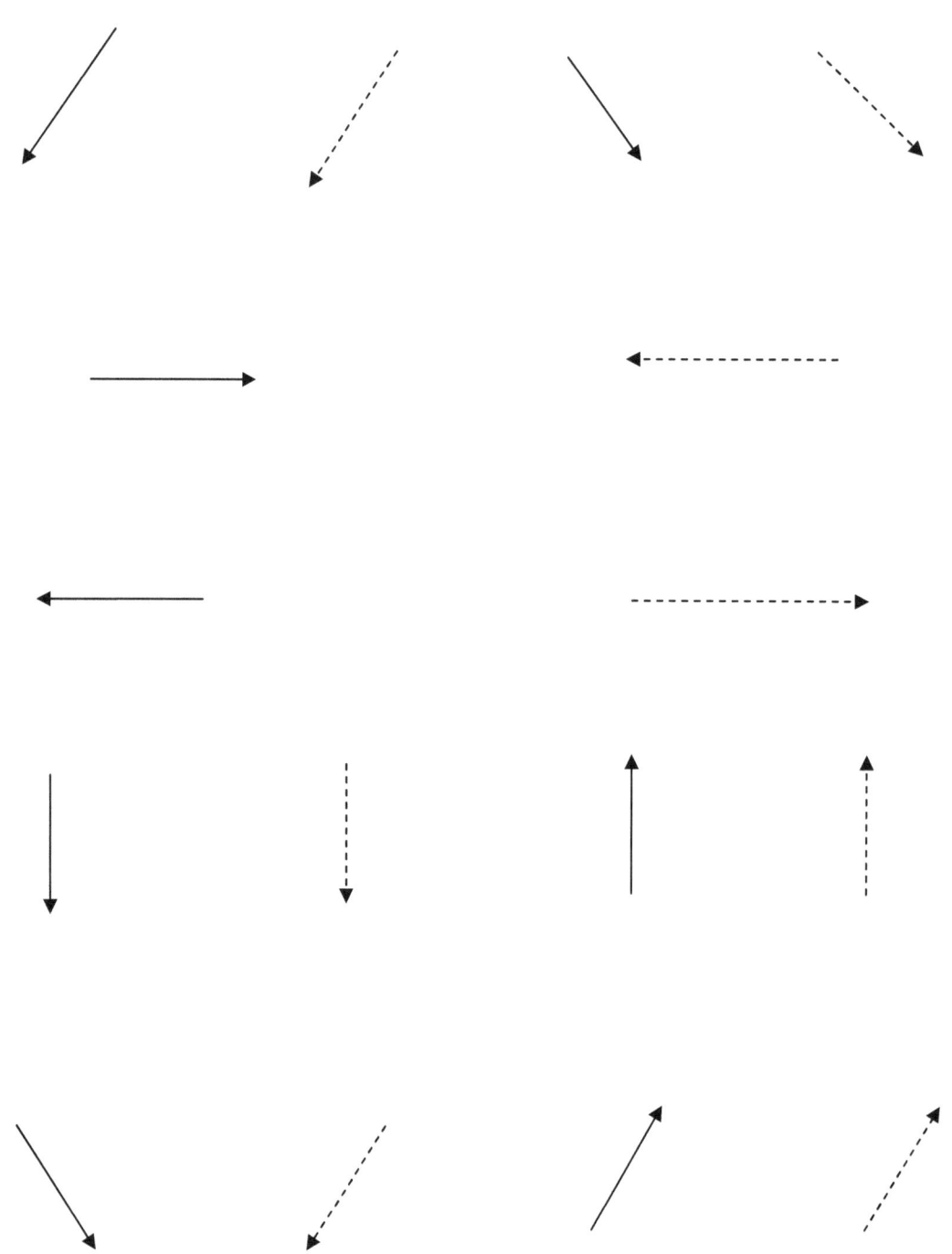

44

Reviewing Shapes

Trace each shape

Color the shapes

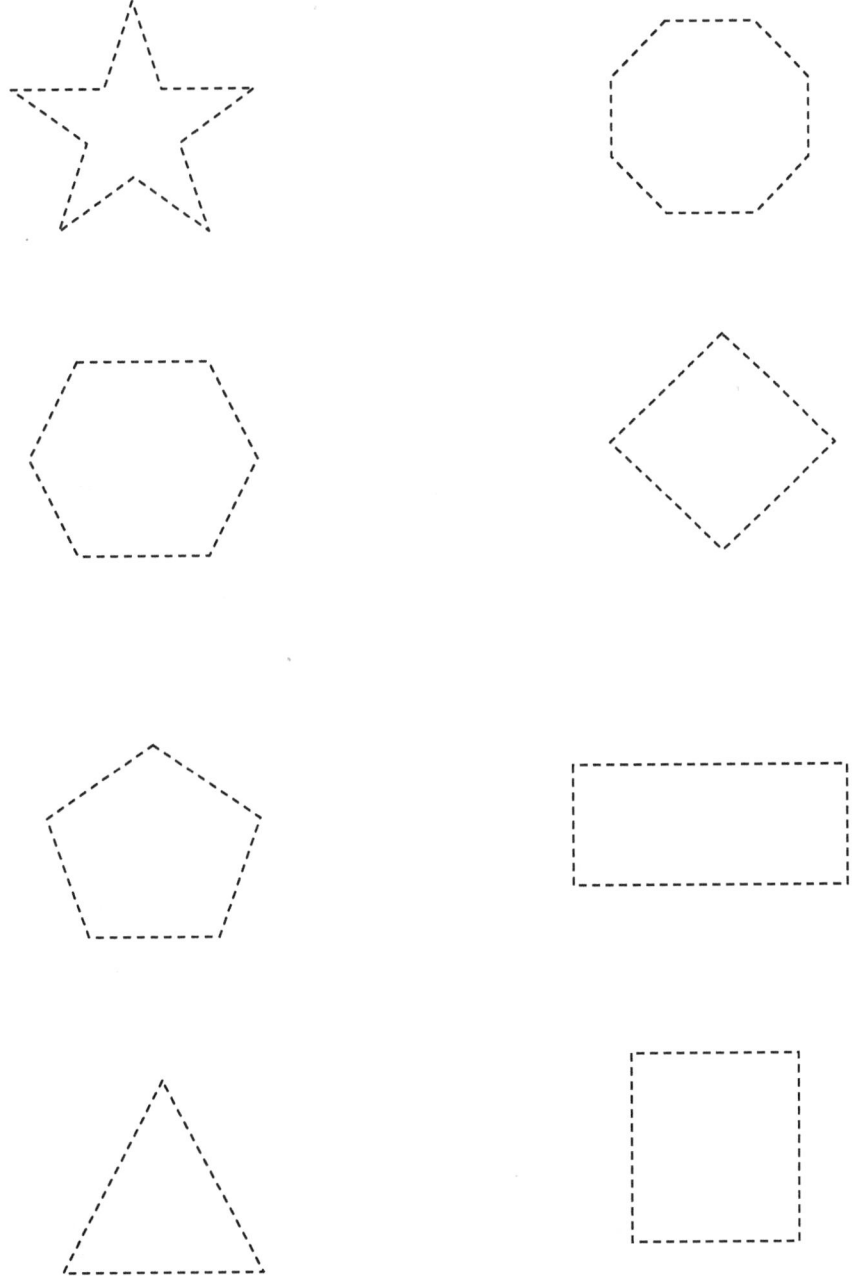

Follow the arrows to form arches using a gray crayon

Trace the arches using a gray crayon

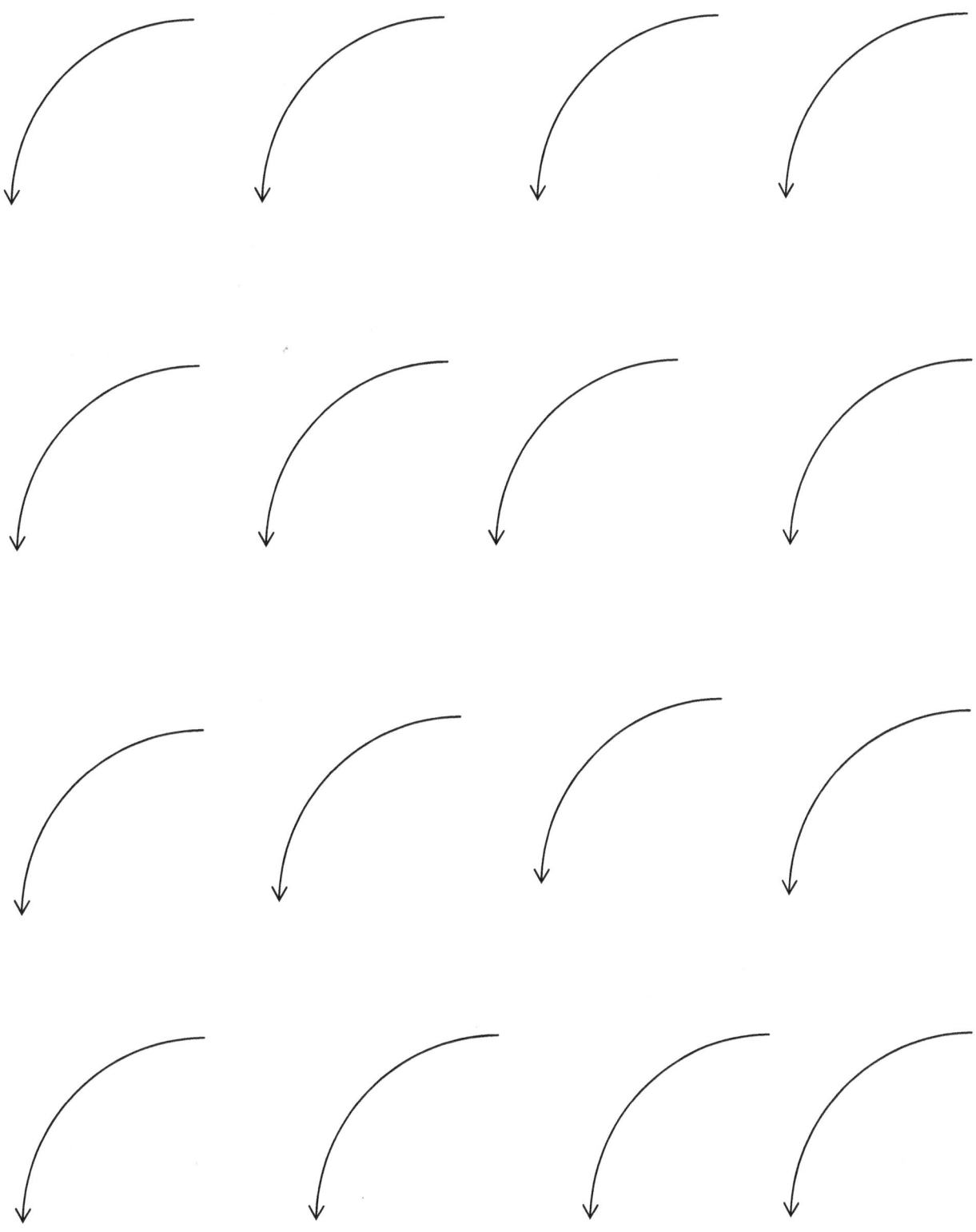

Draw arches using a gray crayon

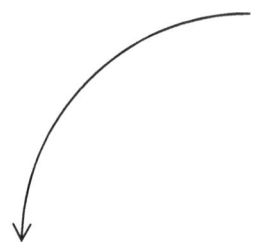

Follow the arrows to form arches using a gray crayon

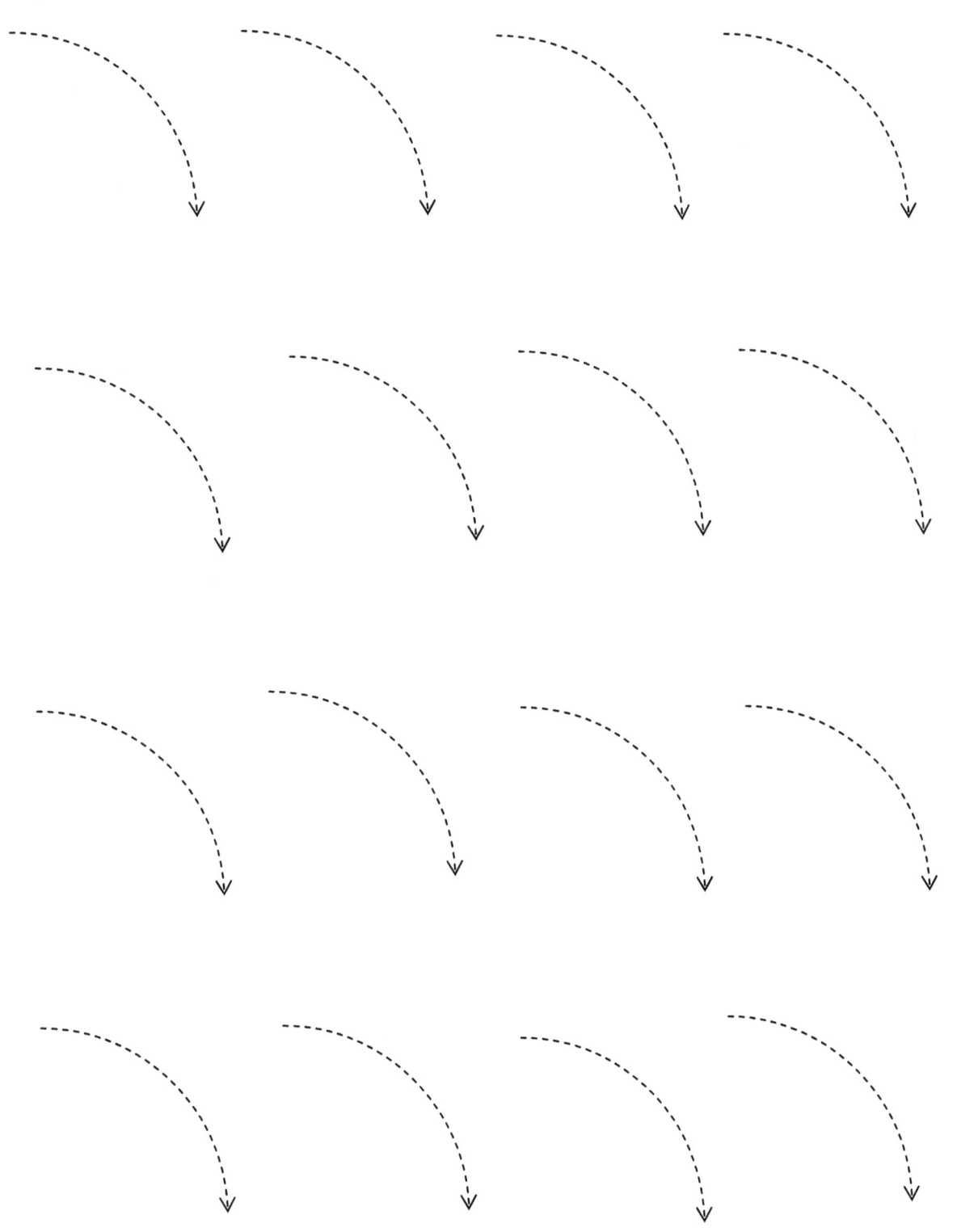

Trace the arches using a gray crayon

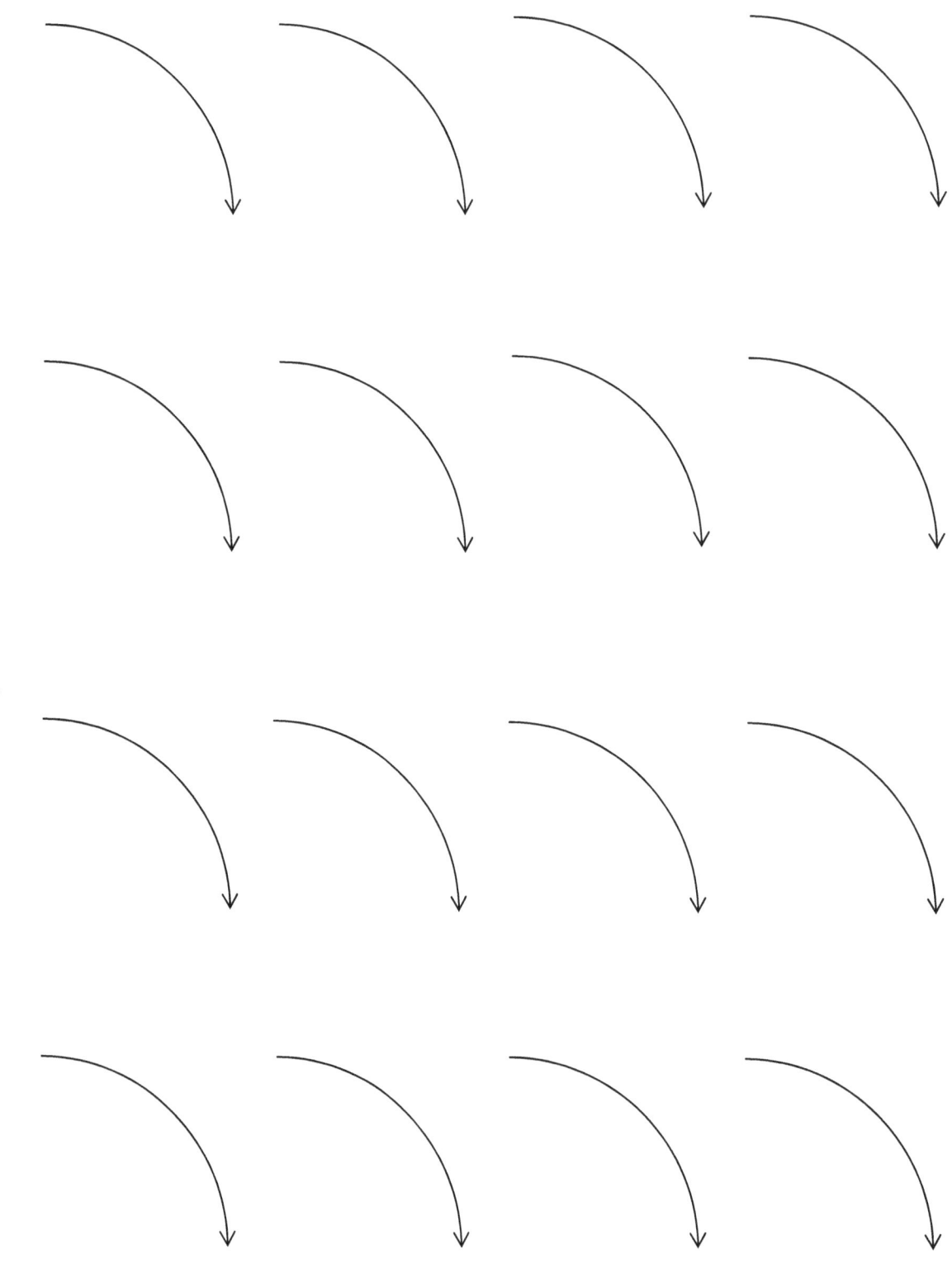

Draw arches using a gray crayon

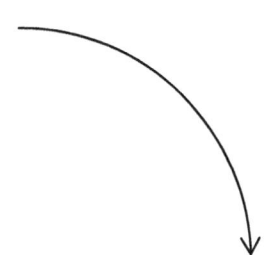

Drawing Circles

Follow the arrows to form arches using a black crayon

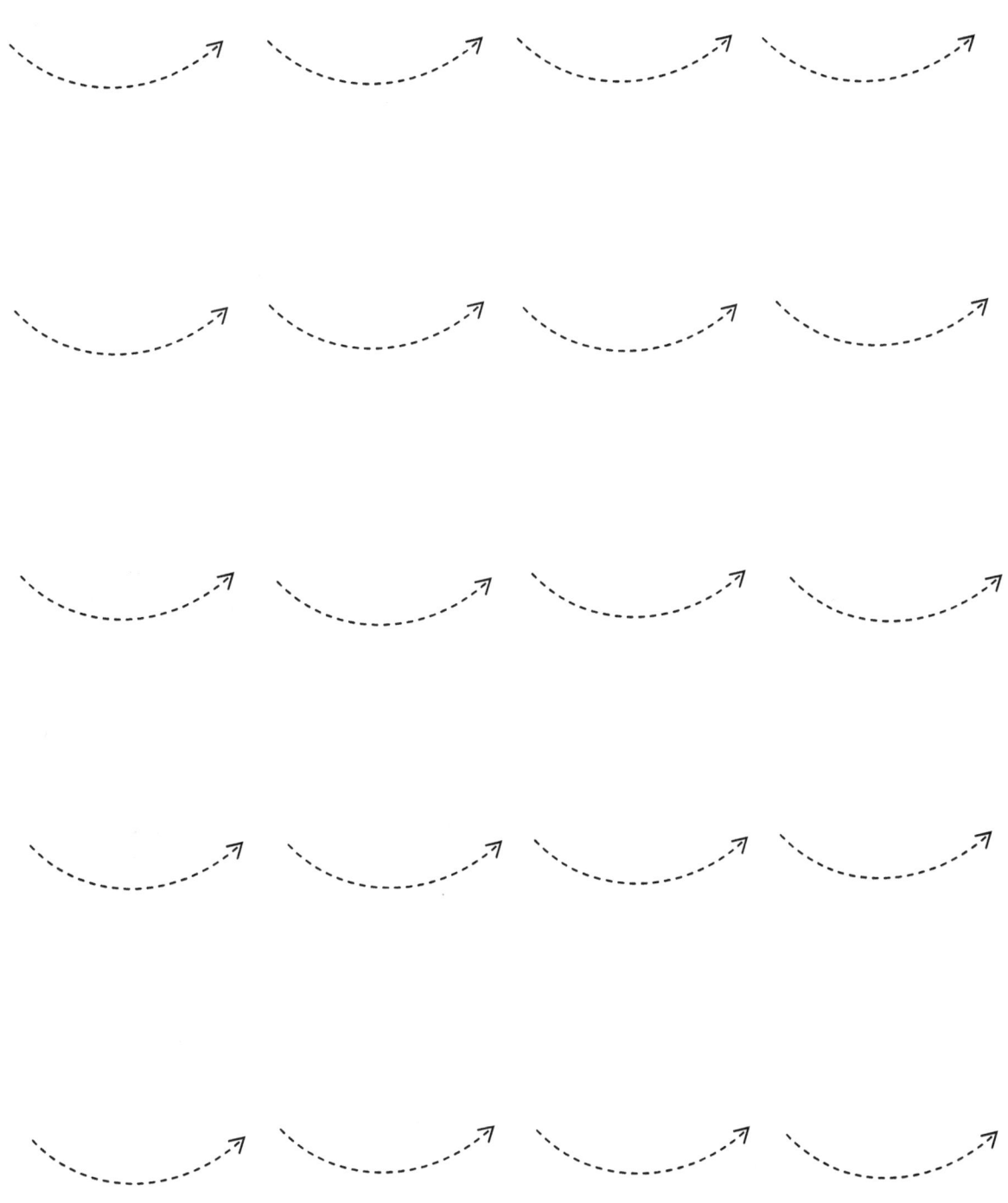

Trace the arrows to form arches using a black crayon

Draw arches using a black crayon

Follow the arrows to form arches using a black crayon

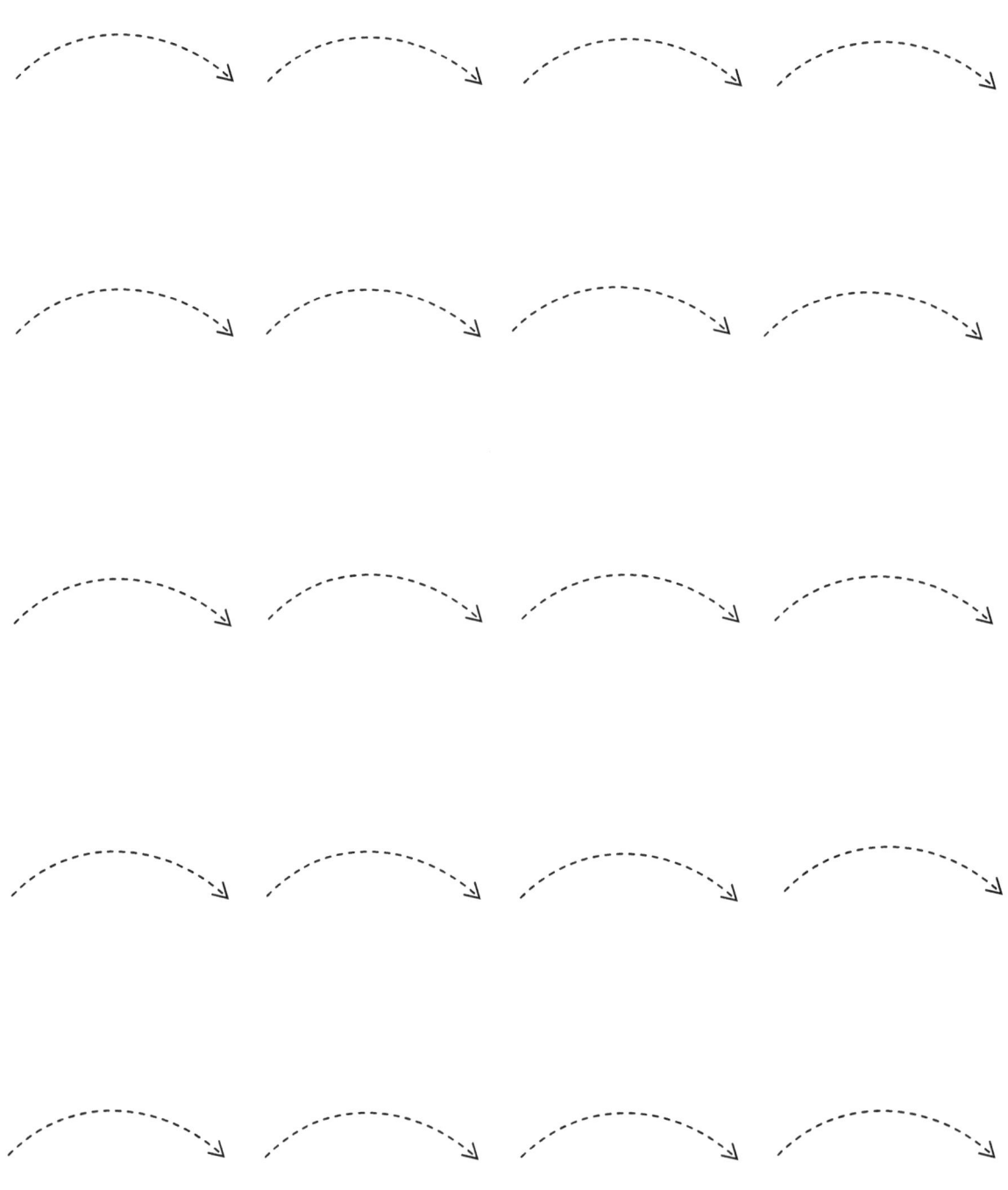

Trace the arches using a black crayon

Draw arches using a black crayon

Drawing Ovals

59

REVIEWING LINES AND ARCHES

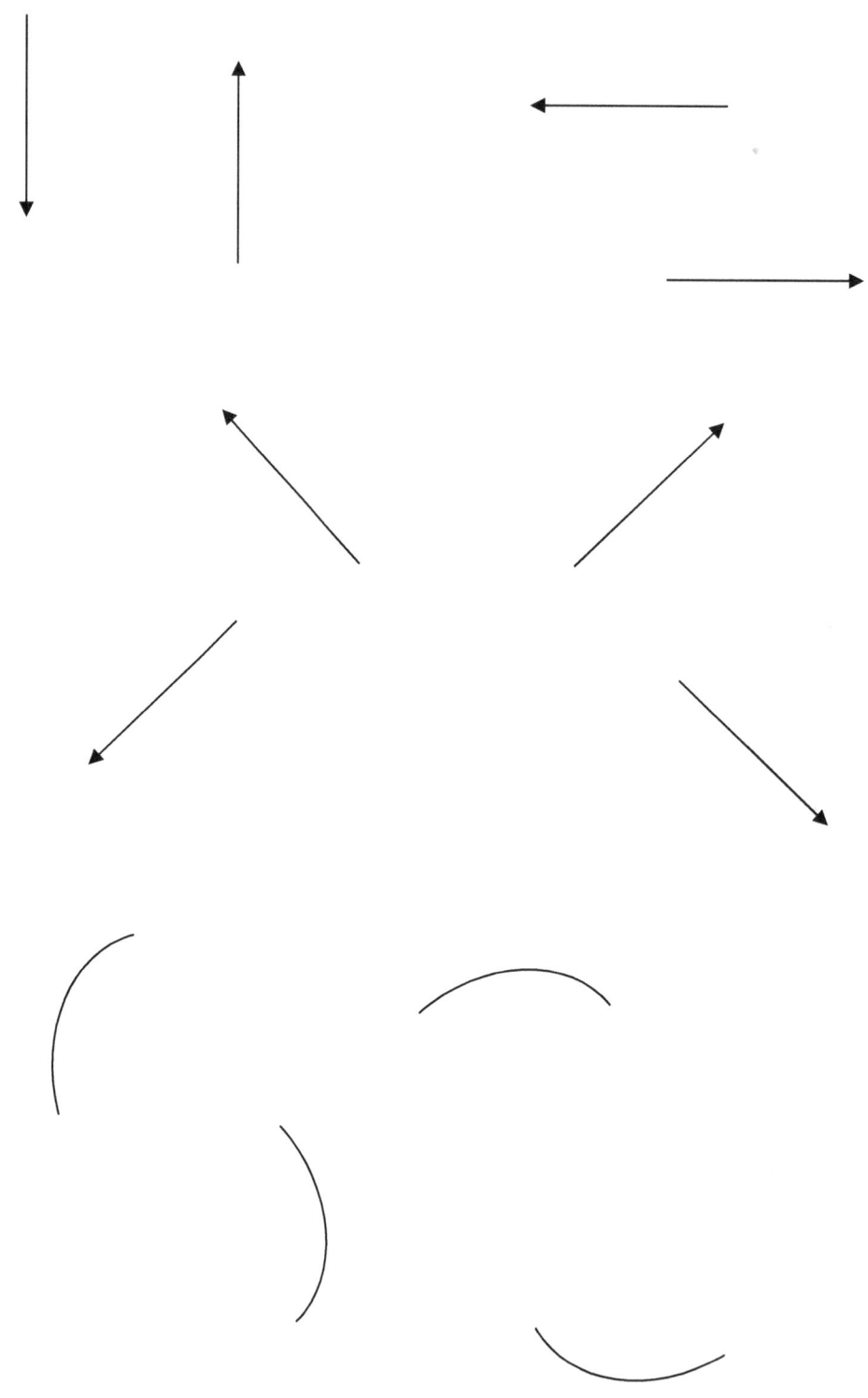

Drawing Hearts

REVIEWING ALL SHAPES

Color each shape a different color

Writing

A to Z

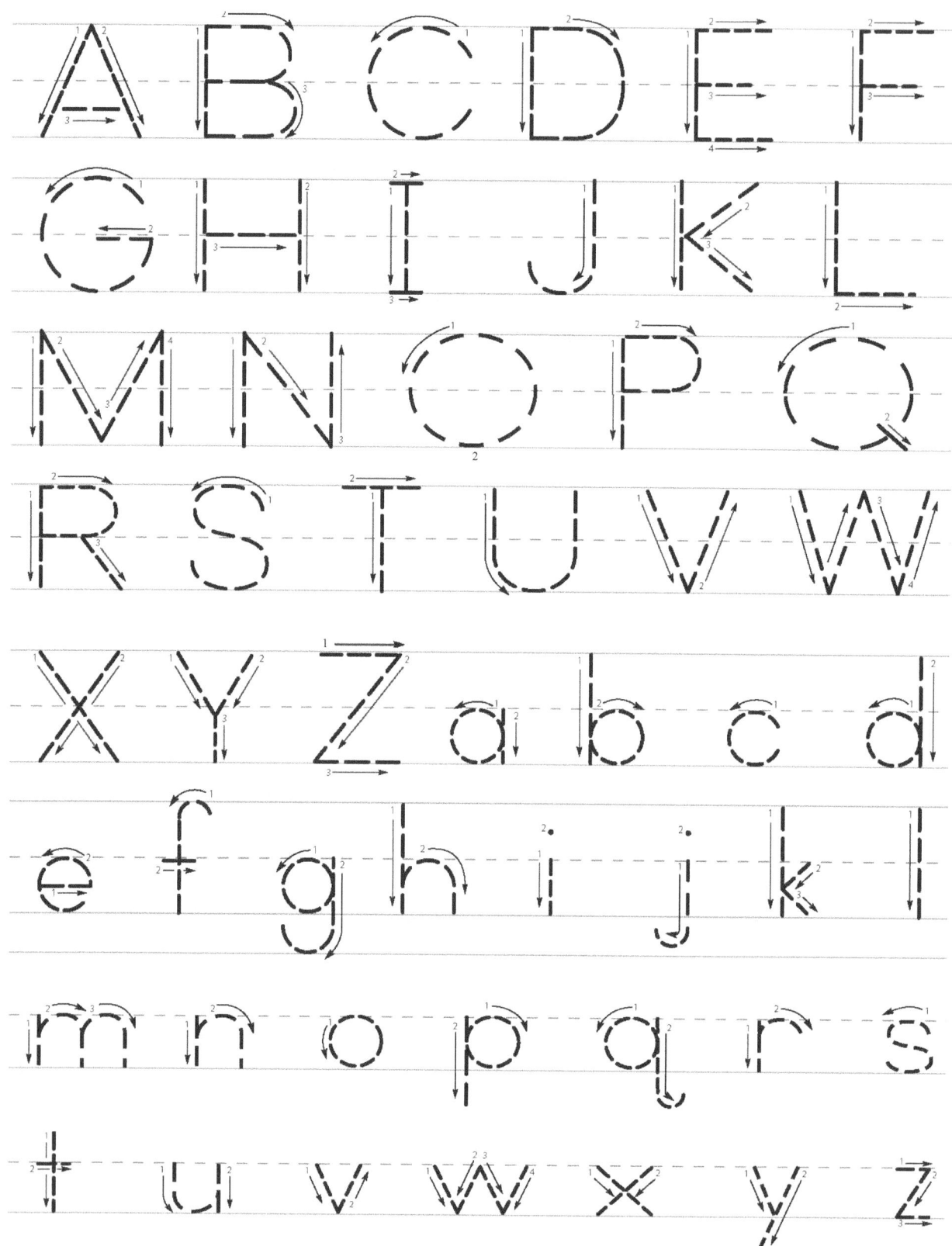

A   a

B						b

C   C

D	d

E						e

F   f

G						g

H   h

I   i

J j

K   k

L | I

M   m

N   n

O   O

P			p

Q   q

R   r

S   s

T   t

U   U

V

V

W   W

X   X

Y   y

Z   Z

Writing

One to Ten

1:10

One

1

Two
2

Three

3

Four
4

Five

5

Six

6

Seven

7

Eight

8

Nine

9

Ten

10

Math

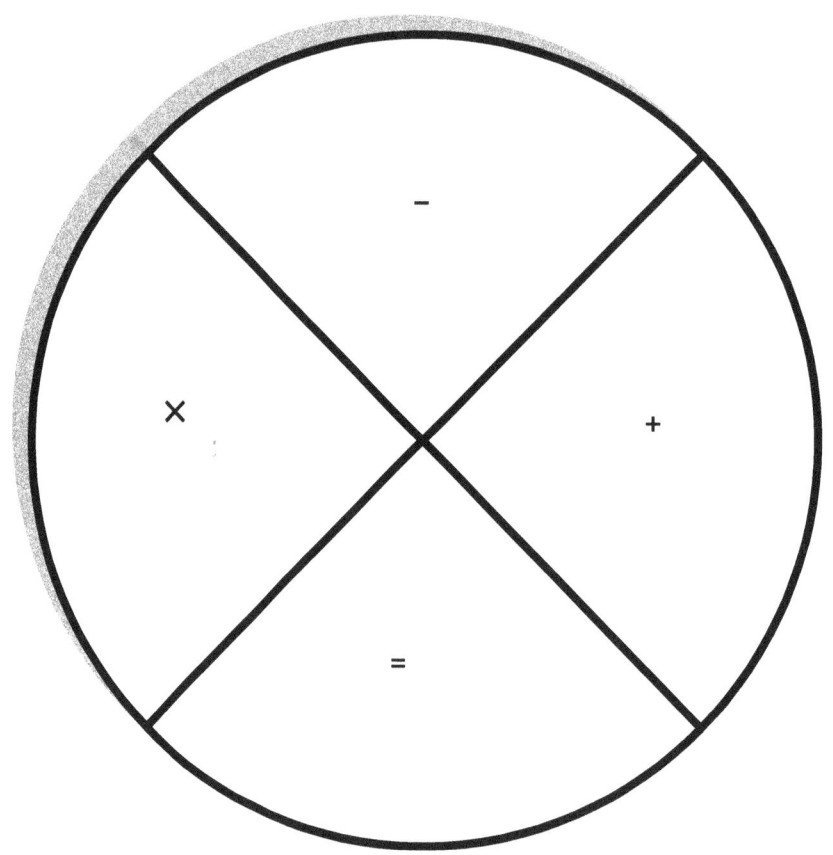

Equals 10

Write two equations for each set of problems
Example:

9 + 1 = 10

1 + 9 = 10

___ + ___ = 10

___ + ___ = 10

_____ + _____ = 10

_____ + _____ = 10

____ + ____ = 10
____ + ____ = 10

____ + ____ = 10

____ + ____ = 10

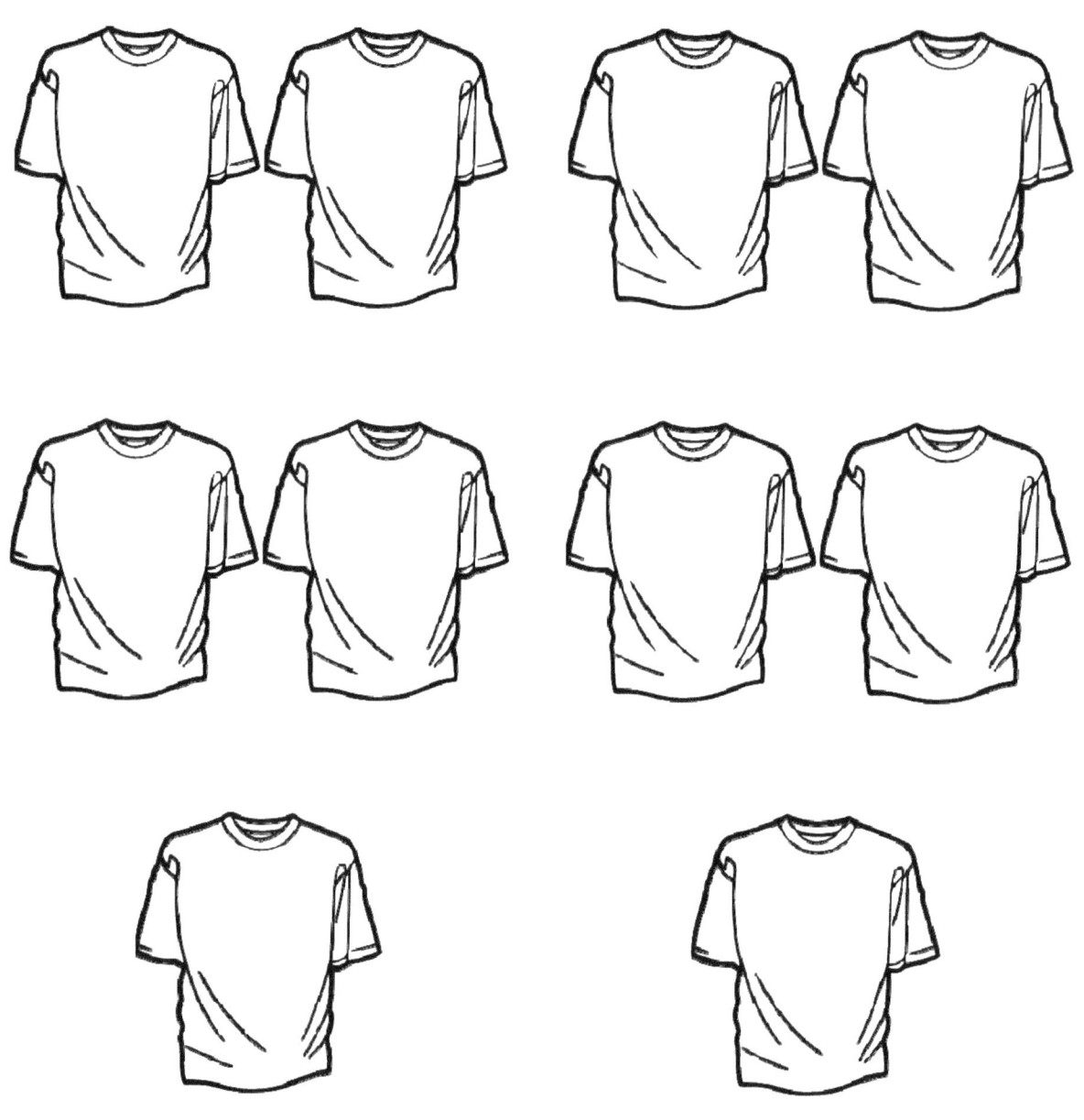

____ + ____ = 10

____ + ____ = 10

Subtracting 10

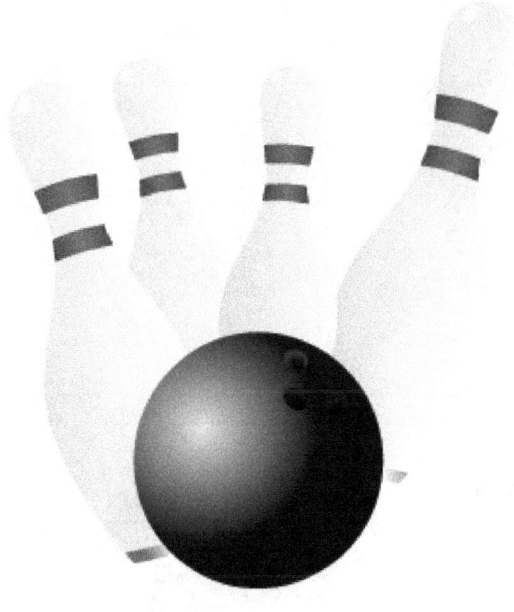

Place at x over the correct number of objects to solve each equation

$10 - 0 =$

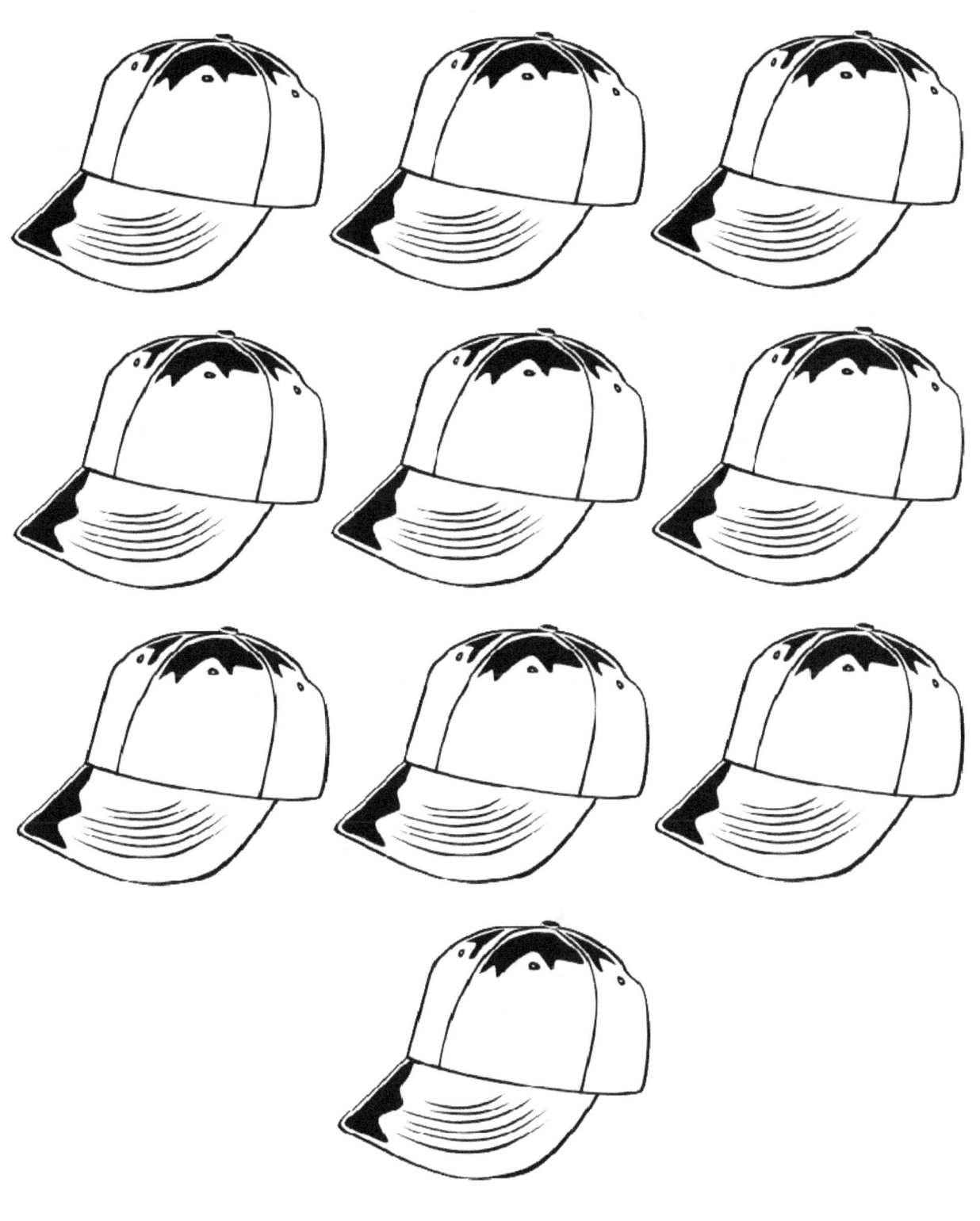

$10 - 1 =$

$10 - 2 =$

$10 - 3 =$

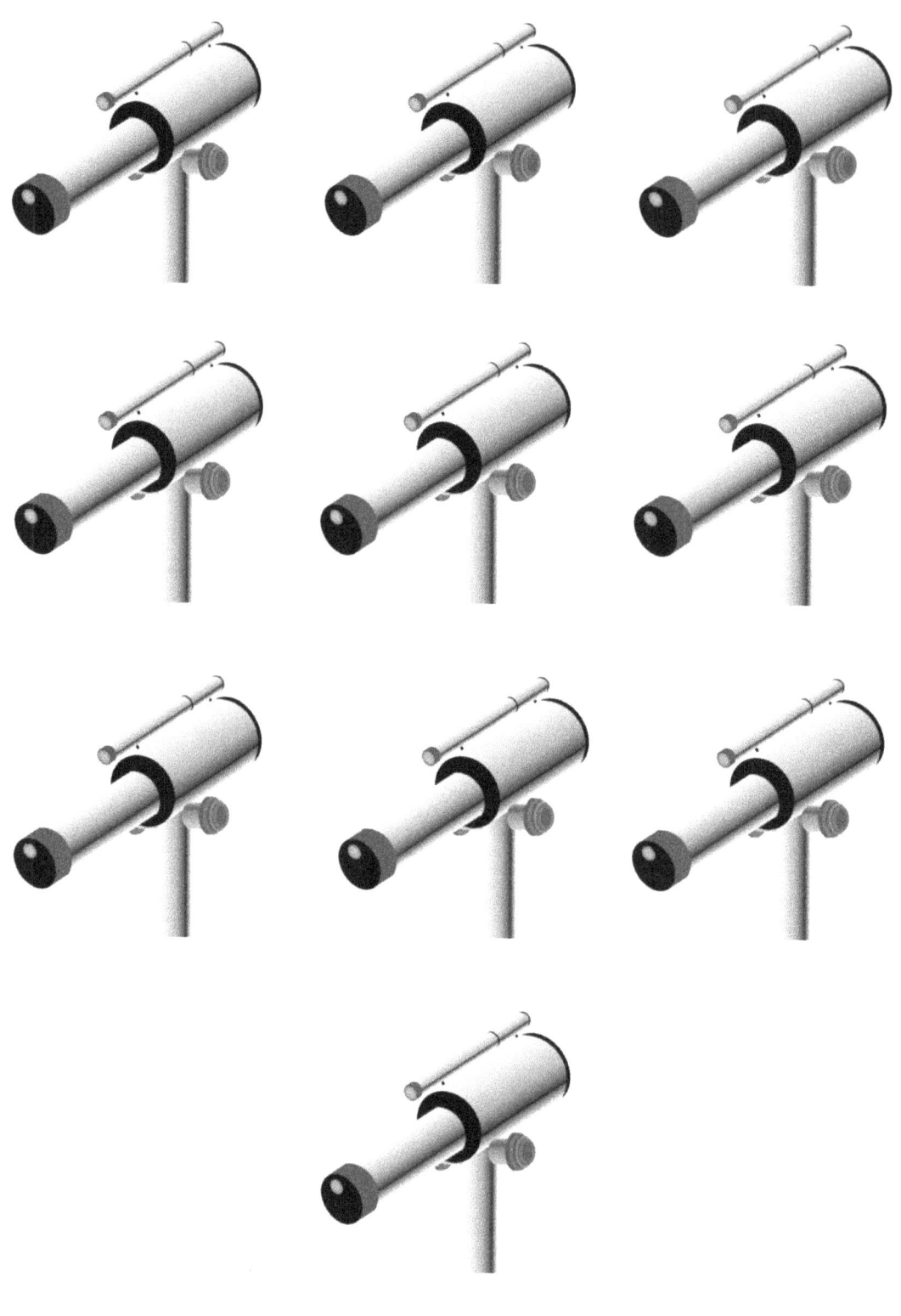

10 − 4 =

10 − 5 =

$10 - 6 =$

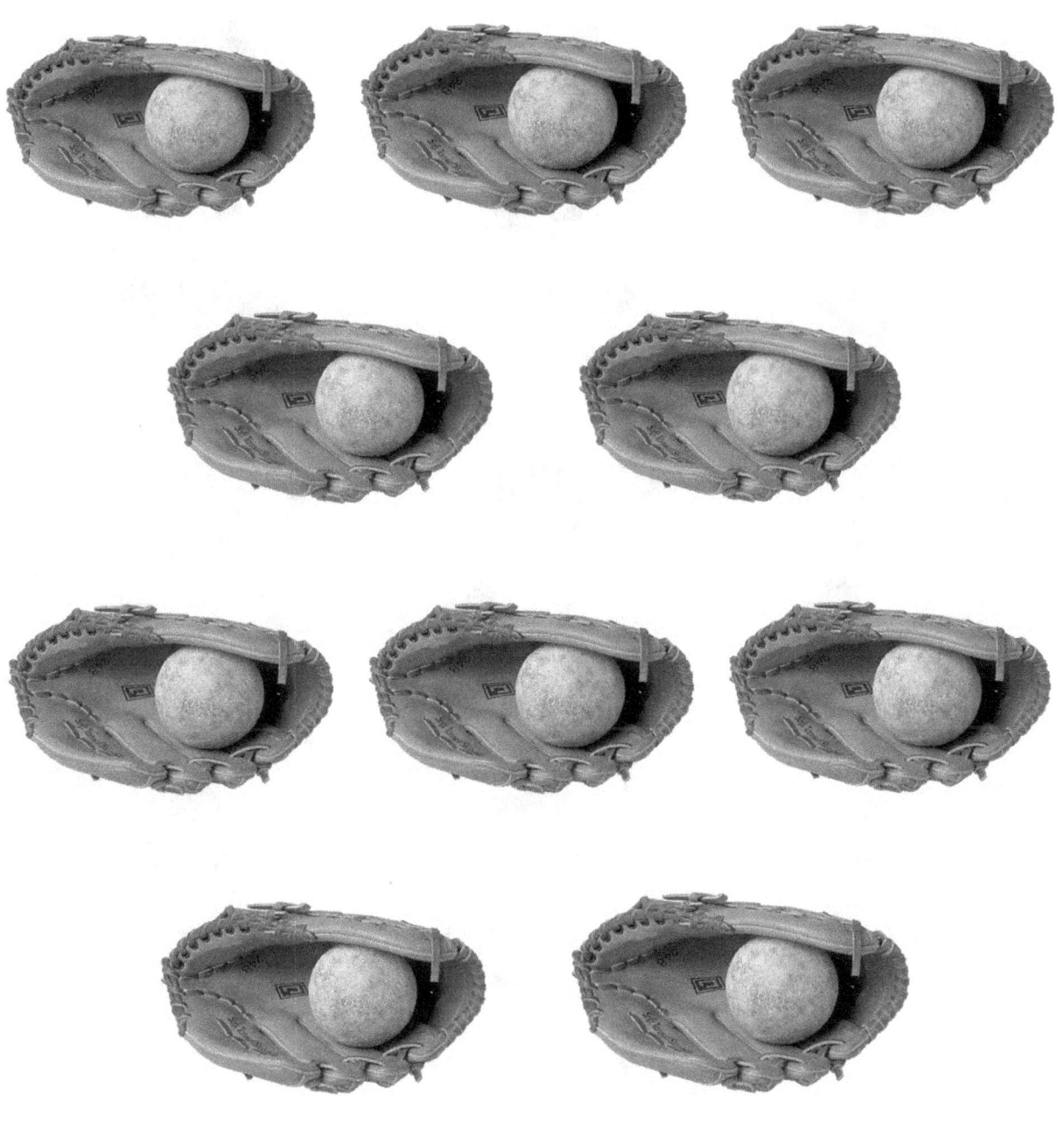

10 − 7 =

10 − 8 =

$10 - 9 =$

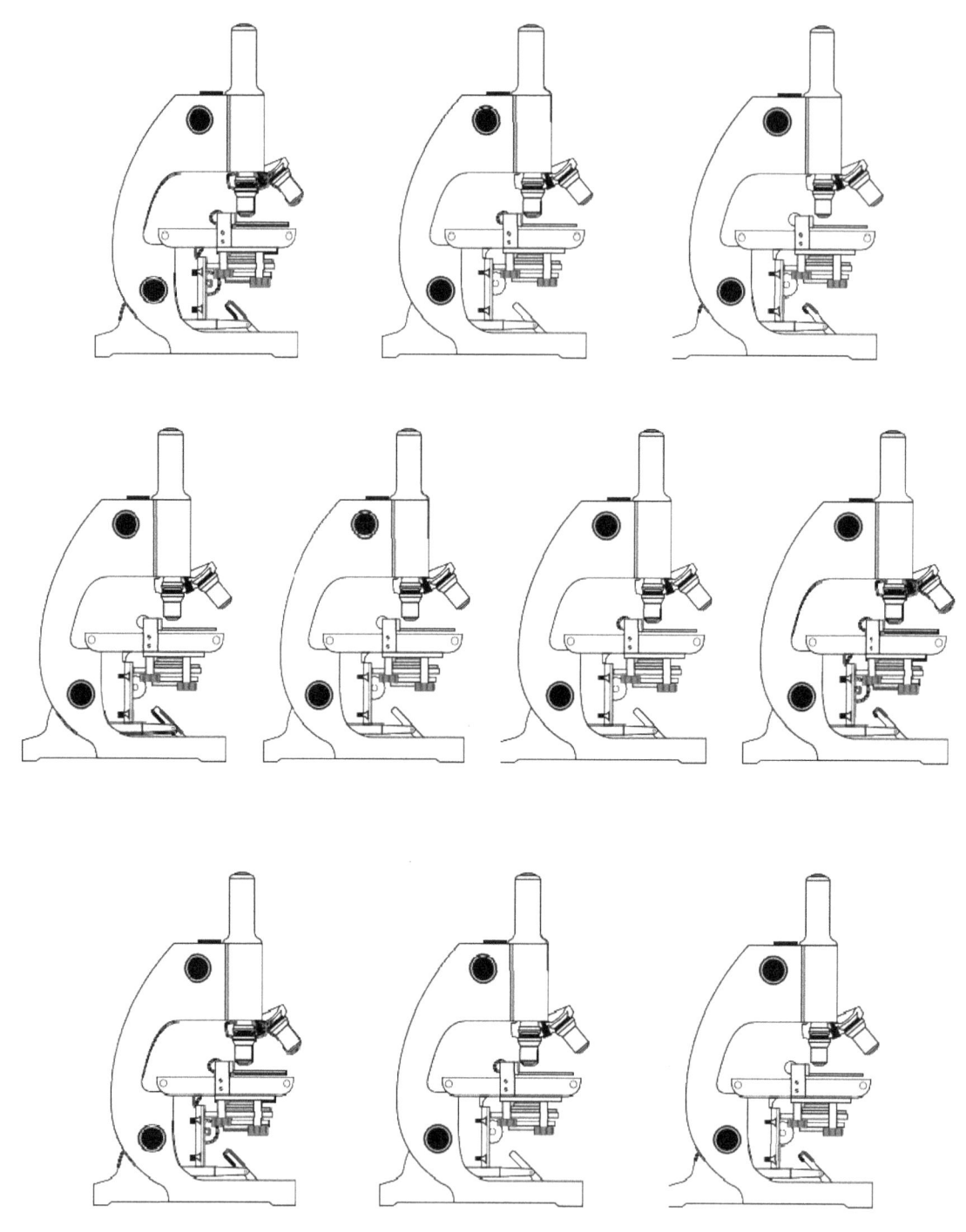

$10 - 10 =$

Eleven	To	Nineteen
11	Eleven	eleven
12	Twelve	twelve
13	Thirteen	thirteen
14	Fourteen	fourteen
15	Fifteen	fifteen
16	Sixteen	sixteen
17	Seventeen	seventeen
18	Eighteen	eighteen
19	Nineteen	nineteen

Match the Number to the Word

11	eleven	Eleven
13	thirteen	Thirteen
15	twelve	Twelve
12	fourteen	Fourteen
14	fifteen	Fifteen
16	seventeen	Seventeen
19	eighteen	Eighteen
18	sixteen	Sixteen
17	nineteen	Nineteen

Draw circles in the boxes for each number

11	
12	
13	
14	
15	
16	
17	
18	
19	

Write the word for each number

11 _____ _____ _____

12 _____ _____ _____

13 _____ _____ _____

14 _____ _____ _____

15 _____ _____ _____

16 _____ _____ _____

17 _____ _____ _____

18 _____ _____ _____

19 _____ _____ _____

Counting to 19

Fill in the square with the correct numbers

0				

			3	

5				

		7		

		17		

15				

	6			

0				
	16			

				4

Draw circles in each box to solve the equation

```
   0
+ 20  =  [        ]   +   [        ]

   1
+ 19  =  [        ]   +   [        ]

   2
+ 18  =  [        ]   +   [        ]

   3
+ 17  =  [        ]   +   [        ]

   4
+ 16  =  [        ]   +   [        ]
```

Draw circles in each box to solve the equation

   5
+ 15 = [ ]   +   [ ]

   6
+ 14 = [ ]   +   [ ]

   7
+ 13 = [ ]   +   [ ]

   8
+ 12 = [ ]   +   [ ]

   9
+ 11 = [ ]   +   [ ]

Draw circles in each box to solve equation

15
+ 5 = ☐   +   ☐

16
+ 4 = ☐   +   ☐

17
+ 3 = ☐   +   ☐

18
+ 2 = ☐   +   ☐

19
+ 1 = ☐   +   ☐

Draw circles in each box to solve the equation

10
+ 10 = [   ]   +   [   ]

11
+ 9   = [   ]   +   [   ]

12
+ 8   = [   ]   +   [   ]

13
+ 7   = [   ]   +   [   ]

14
+ 6   = [   ]   +   [   ]

ADDING TO 20

0 + 20 = ____   10 + 10 = ____

1 + 19 = ____   11 + 9 = ____

2 + 18 = ____   12 + 8 = ____

3 + 17 = ____   13 + 7 = ____

4 + 16 = ____   14 + 6 = ____

5 + 15 = ____   15 + 5 = ____

6 + 14 = ____   16 + 4 = ____

7 + 13 = ____   17 + 3 = ____

8 + 12 = ____   18 + 2 = ____

9 + 11 = ____   19 + 1 = ____

Challenge Question:
Tevin needs 20 books to fill up his bookcase. He already has 10. DeRell gave him 3 books. How many more books does Tevin need to reach his goal?

Basic Addition

1 + 0 = ____   2 + 2 = ____

1 + 1 = ____   2 + 3 = ____

1 + 2 = ____   2 + 4 = ____

1 + 3 = ____   2 + 5 = ____

1 + 4 = ____   2 + 6 = ____

1 + 5 = ____   2 + 7 = ____

1 + 6 = ____   2 + 8 = ____

1 + 7 = ____   2 + 9 = ____

1 + 8 = ____   2 + 10 = ____

1 + 9 = ____   3 + 0 = ____

1 + 10 = ____   3 + 1 = ____

2 + 0 = ____   3 + 2 = ____

2 + 1 = ____   3 + 3 = ____

3 + 4 = ____

3 + 5 = ____

3 + 6 = ____

3 + 7 = ____

3 + 8 = ____

3 + 9 = ____

3 + 10 = ____

4 + 0 = ____

4 + 1 = ____

4 + 2 = ____

4 + 3 = ____

4 + 4 = ____

4 + 5 = ____

4 + 6 = ____

4 + 7 = ____

4 + 8 = ____

4 + 9 = ____

4 + 10 = ____

5 + 0 = ____

5 + 1 = ____

5 + 2 = ____

5 + 3 = ____

5 + 4 = ____

5 + 5 = ____

5 + 6 = ____

5 + 7 = ____

5 + 8 = ____

5 + 9 = ____

5 + 10 = ____

6 + 0 = ____

6 + 1 = ____

6 + 2 = ____

6 + 3 = ____

6 + 4 = ____

6 + 5 = ____

6 + 6 = ____

6 + 7 = ____

6 + 8 = ____

6 + 9 = ____

6 + 10 = ____

7 + 0 = ____

7 + 1 = ____

7 + 2 = ____

7 + 3 = ____

7 + 4 = ____

7 + 5 = ____

7 + 6 = ____

7 + 7 = ____

7 + 8 = ____

7 + 9 = ____

7 + 10 = ____

8 + 0 = ____

8 + 1 = ____

8 + 2 = ____

8 + 3 = ____

8 + 4 = ____

8 + 5 = ____

8 + 6 = ____

8 + 7 = ____

8 + 8 = ____

8 + 9 = ____

8 + 10 = ____

9 + 0 = ____

9 + 1 = ____

9 + 2 = ____

9 + 3 = ____

9 + 4 = ____

9 + 5 = ____

9 + 6 = ____

9 + 7 = ____

9 + 8 = ____

9 + 9 = ____

9 + 10 = ____

10 + 0 = ____

10 + 1 = ____

10 + 2 = ____

10 + 3 = ____

10 + 4 = ____

10 + 5 = ____

10 + 6 = ____

10 + 7 = ____

10 + 8 = ____

10 + 9 = ____

10 + 10 = ____

Basic Subtraction

1−0 = ___

1−1 = ___

2−0 = ___

2−1 = ___

2−2 = ___

3−0 = ___

3−1 = ___

3−2 = ___

3−3 = ___

4−0 = ___

4−1 = ___

4−2 = ___

4−3 = ___

4−4 = ___

5−0 = ___

5−1 = ___

5−2 = ___

5−3 = ___

5−4 = ___

5−5 = ___

6−0 = ___

6−1 = ___

6−2 = ___

6−3 = ___

6−4 = ___

6−5 = ___

6−6 = ___

7−0 = ___

7−1 = ___

7−2 = ___

7−3 = ___

7−4 = ___

7−5 = ___

7−6 = ___

7−7 = ___

8−0 = ___

8−1 = ___

8−2 = ___

8−3 = ___

8−4 = ___

8−5 = ___

8−6 = ____

8−7 = ____

8−8 = ____

9−0 = ____

9−1 = ____

9−2 = ____

9−3 = ____

9−4 = ____

9−5 = ____

9−6 = ____

9−7 = ____

9−8 = ____

9−9 = ____

10−0 = ____

10−1 = ____

10−2 = ____

10−3 = ____

10−4 = ____

10−5 = ____

10−6 = ____

10−7 = ____

10−8 = ____

10−9 = ____

10−10 = ____

Adding Two Digits

```
  22        16        46
 +17       +11       + 51


  15        40        37
 + 13      + 32      + 52


  43        80        86
 + 32      + 19      + 12


  20        79        60
 + 19      + 20      + 16


  63        54        38
 + 24      + 30      + 61
```

Tevin has 16 toy airplanes. De'Rell gave him 10 more for his birthday. How many airplanes does Tevin have altogether?

On Friday, Tevin's mom gave him $7. His dad gave him $6 dollars on Saturday. How much money does Tevin have now?

There are 16 students sitting in chairs and 13 students sitting on rugs. How many students are there in all?

Marie read 8 books in August. She read 10 books in September. How many books did Marie read in two months?

Subtracting Two Digits

```
  34        56        64
- 22      - 11      - 51


  25        72        12
- 24      - 41      - 10


  79        29        98
- 32      - 19      - 63


  23        79        46
- 13      - 20      - 10


  57        16        48
- 31      - 13      - 41
```

Amiya has 12 dolls. She gives 4 to Indea. How many dolls does Amiya have now?

There are 18 cookies in the bag? Six of them are broken. How many are not broken?

There are 36 students in the classroom. Thirteen of the students leave to go home. How many students are left in the classroom?

Darrell brought 18 books. Eight of the books are about super heroes. How many of the books are about cars?

TEN TO ONE HUNDRED

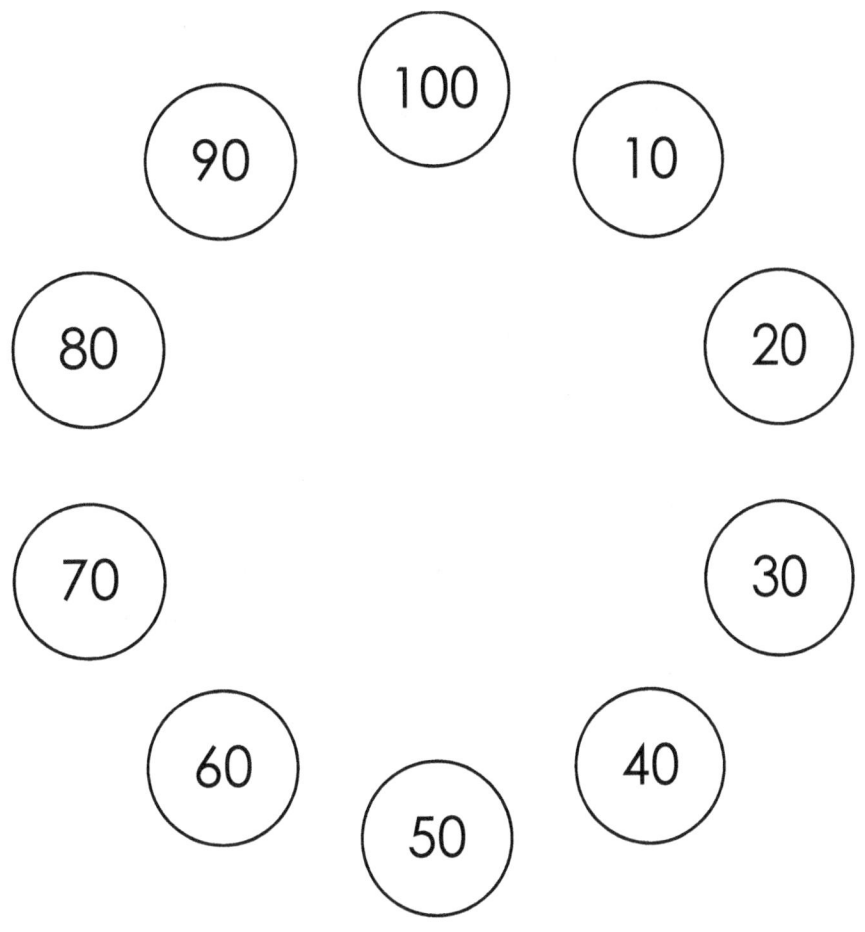

Ten to One Hundred

ten	Ten	10
twenty	Twenty	20
thirty	Thirty	30
forty	Forty	40
fifty	Fifty	50
sixty	Sixty	60
seventy	Seventy	70
eighty	Eighty	80
ninety	Ninety	90
one hundred	One Hundred	100

Write The Word For Each Number

10		
20		
30		
40		
50		
60		
70		
80		
90		
100		

Write The Number

Ten   ten _____

Twenty   twenty _____

Thirty   thirty_____

Forty   forty_____

Fifty   fifty _____

Sixty   sixty_____

Seventy   seventy_____

Eighty   eighty_____

Ninety   ninety_____

One Hundred   one hundred_____

Draw a line from the word to the number

ten	100	Ten
twenty	40	Twenty
thirty	30	Thirty
forty	20	Forty
fifty	10	Fifty
sixty	60	Sixty
seventy	50	Seventy
eighty	90	Eighty
ninety	70	Ninety
one hundred	80	One Hundred

Back To School

By Tens

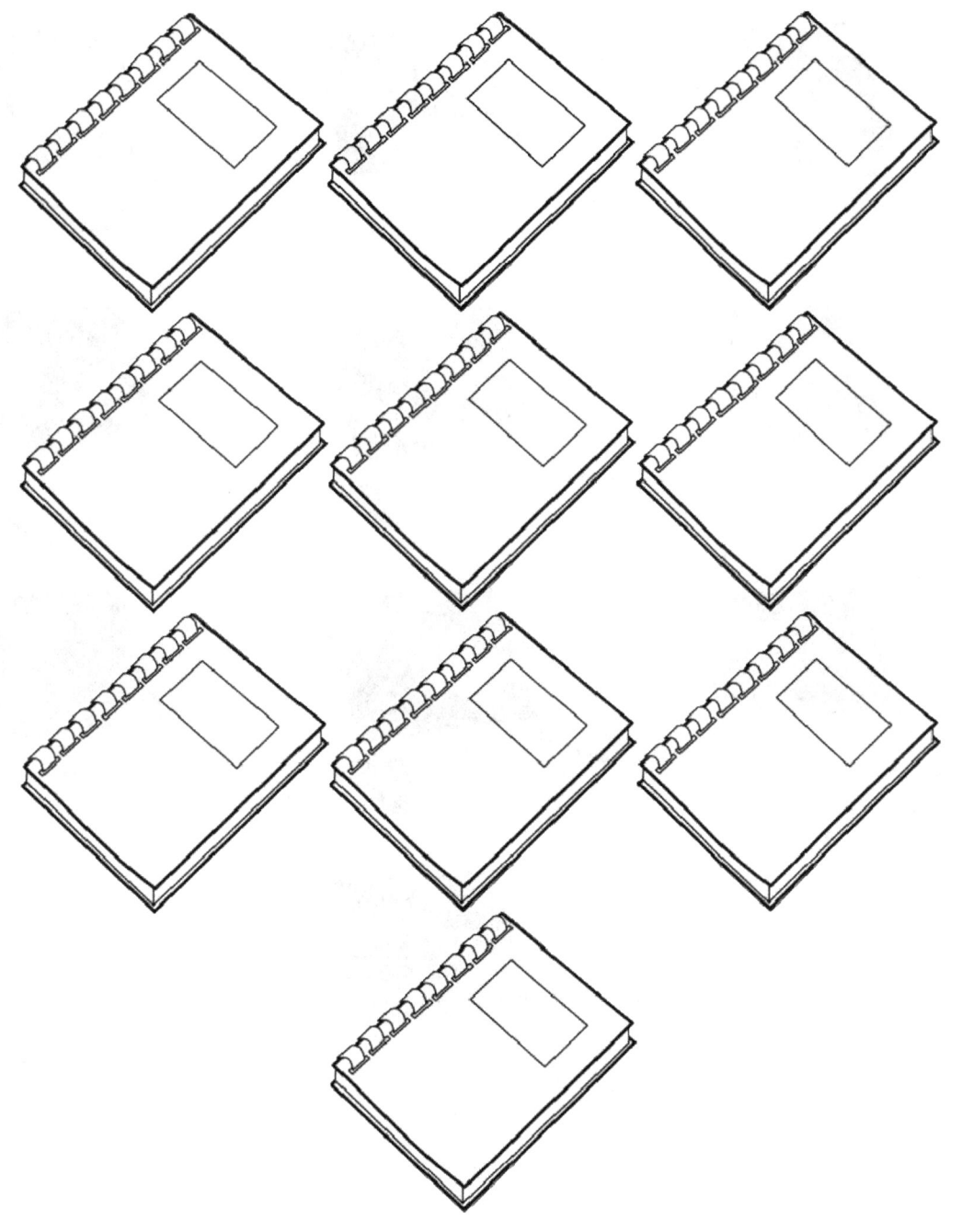

10 notebooks

| | | | | | | | | | 10 |

10
+10 laptops

								20

150

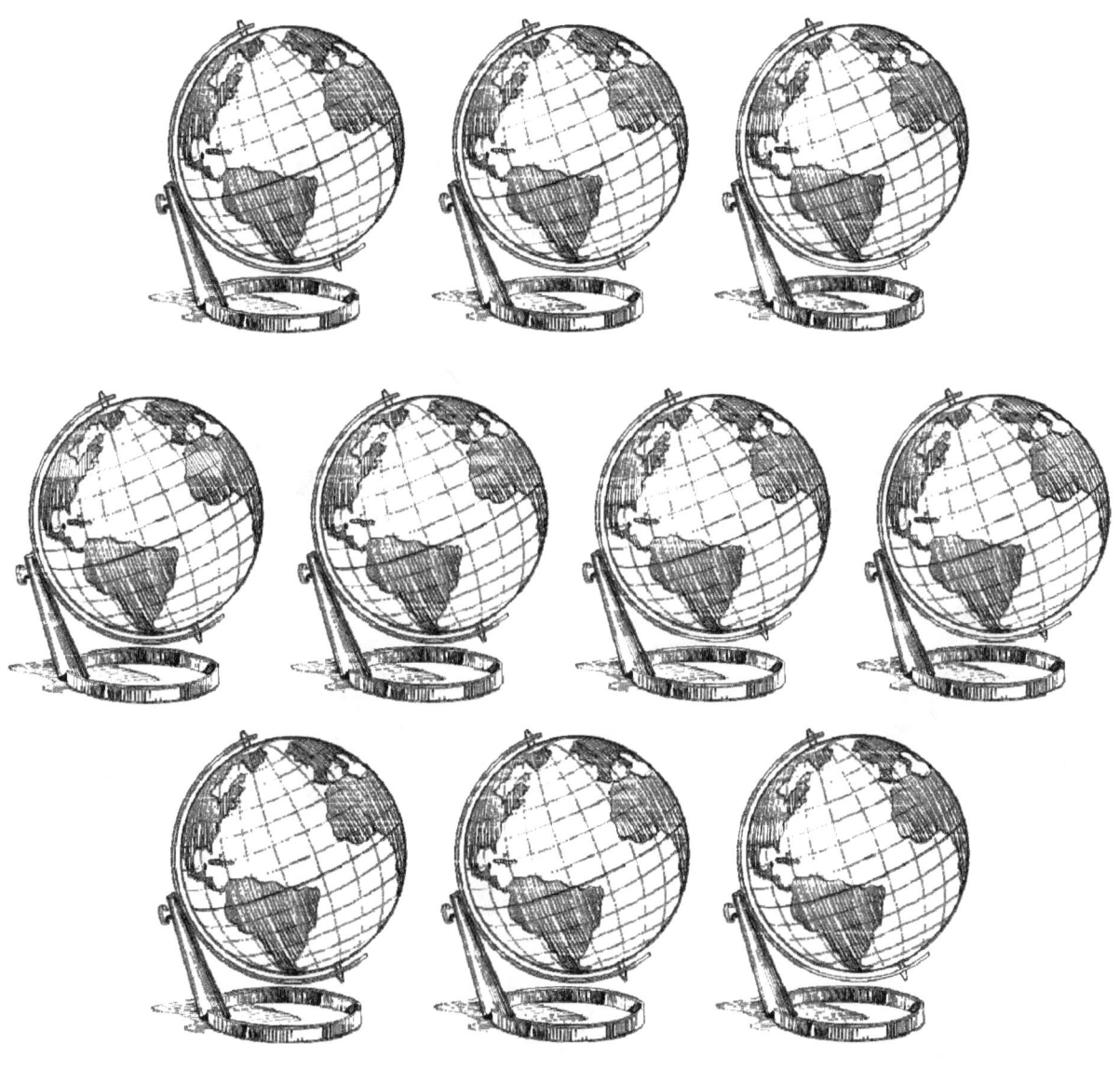

20
+10 globes

| | | | | | | | | | 30 |

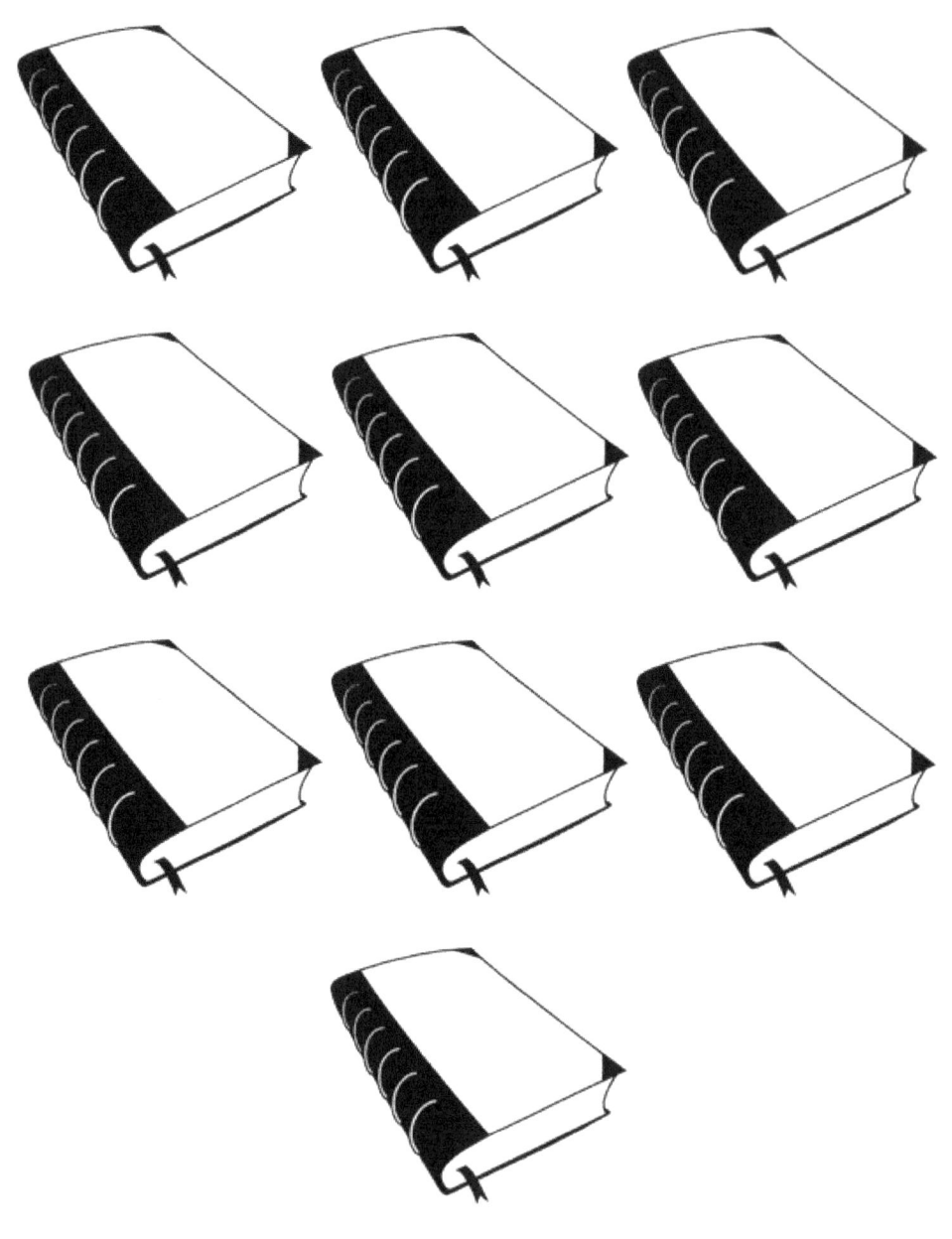

```
  30
+10 books
```

									40

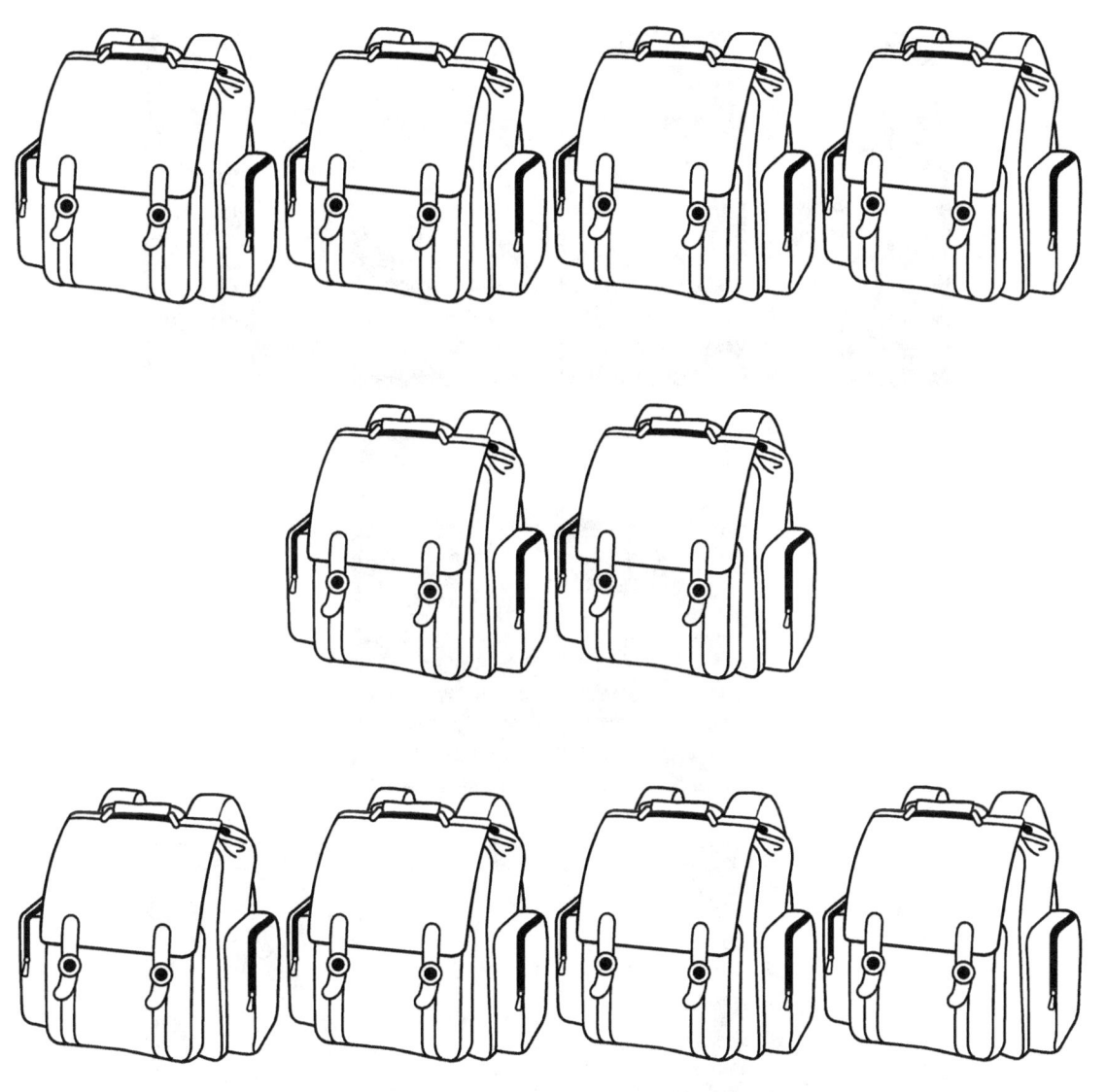

40
+10 book bags

| | | | | | | | | | 50 |

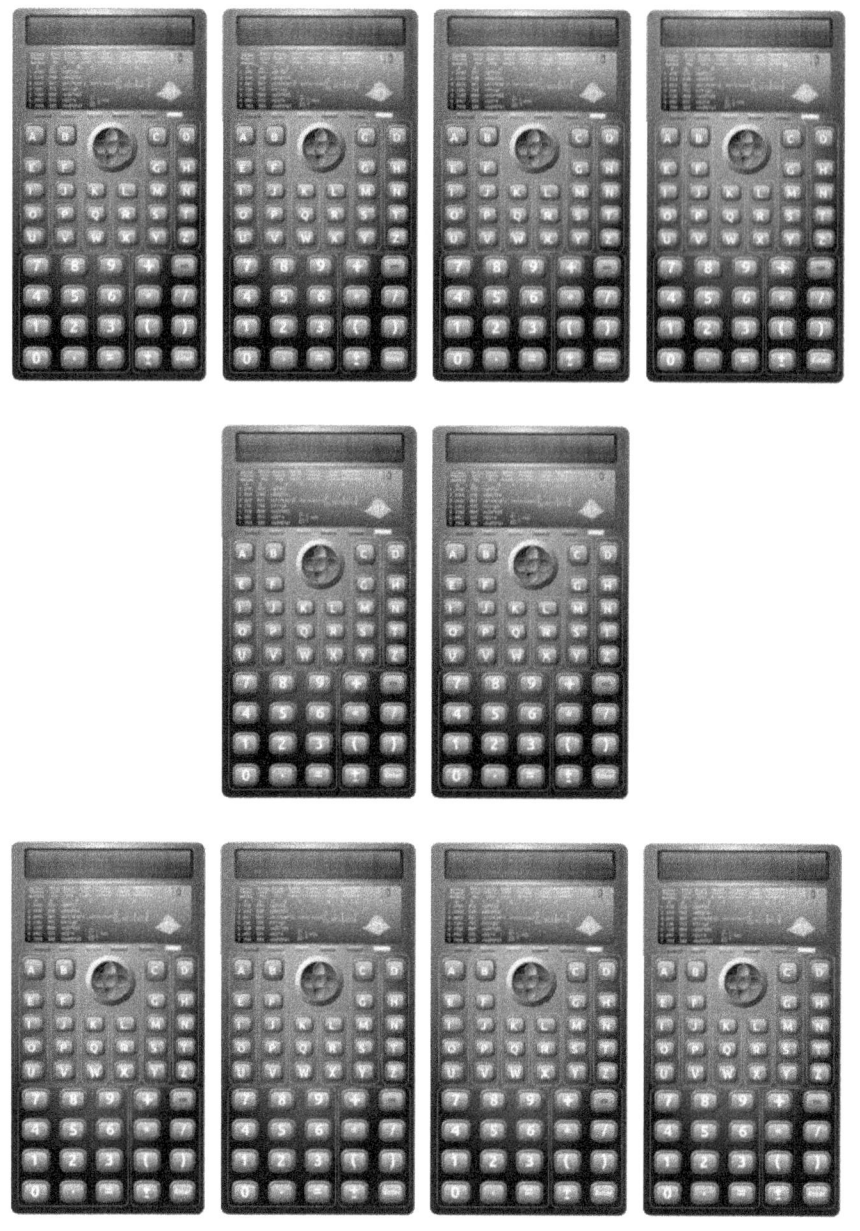

```
  50
+10  calculators
```

									60

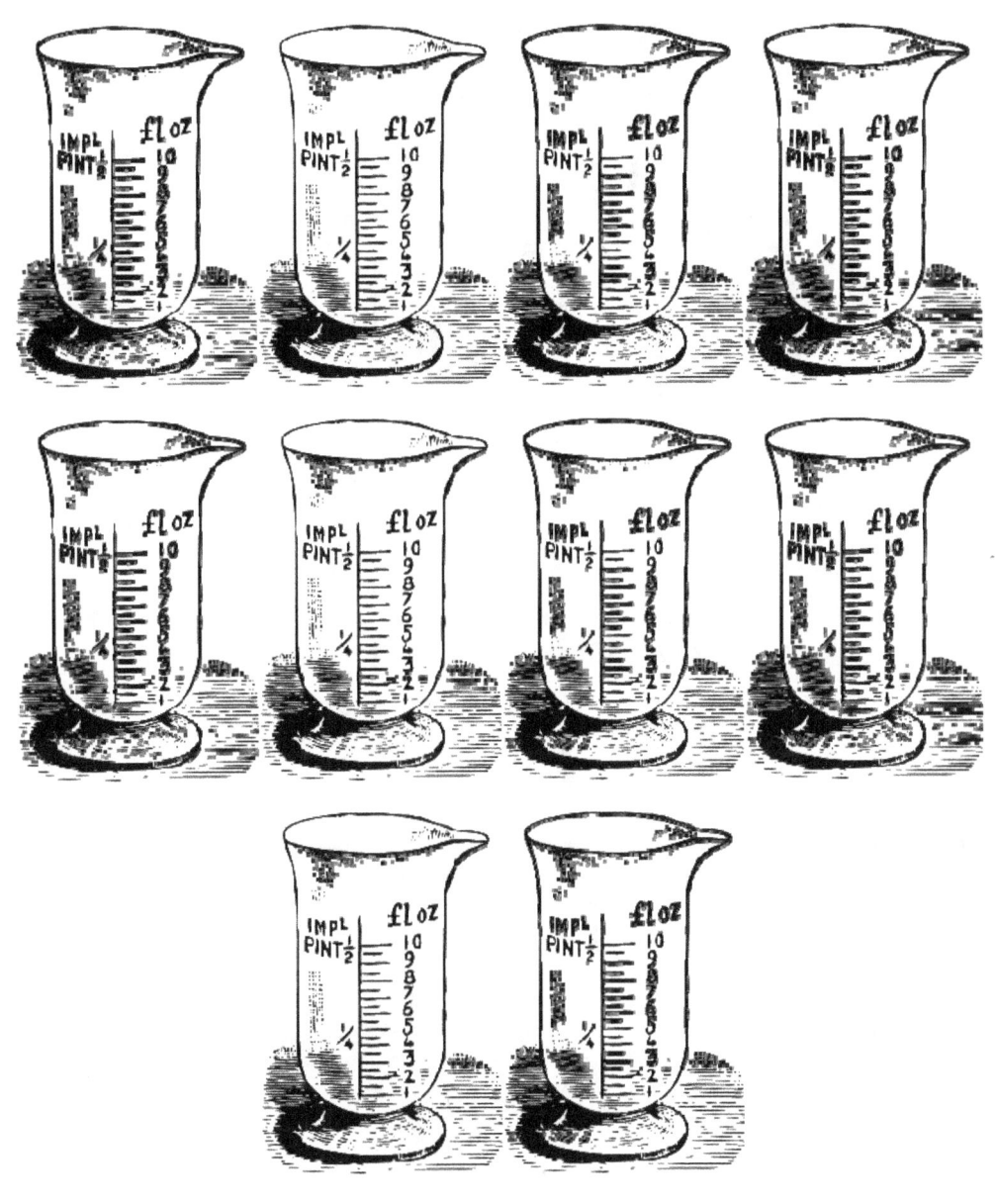

60
+10 measuring cups

									70

70
+10 easels

									80

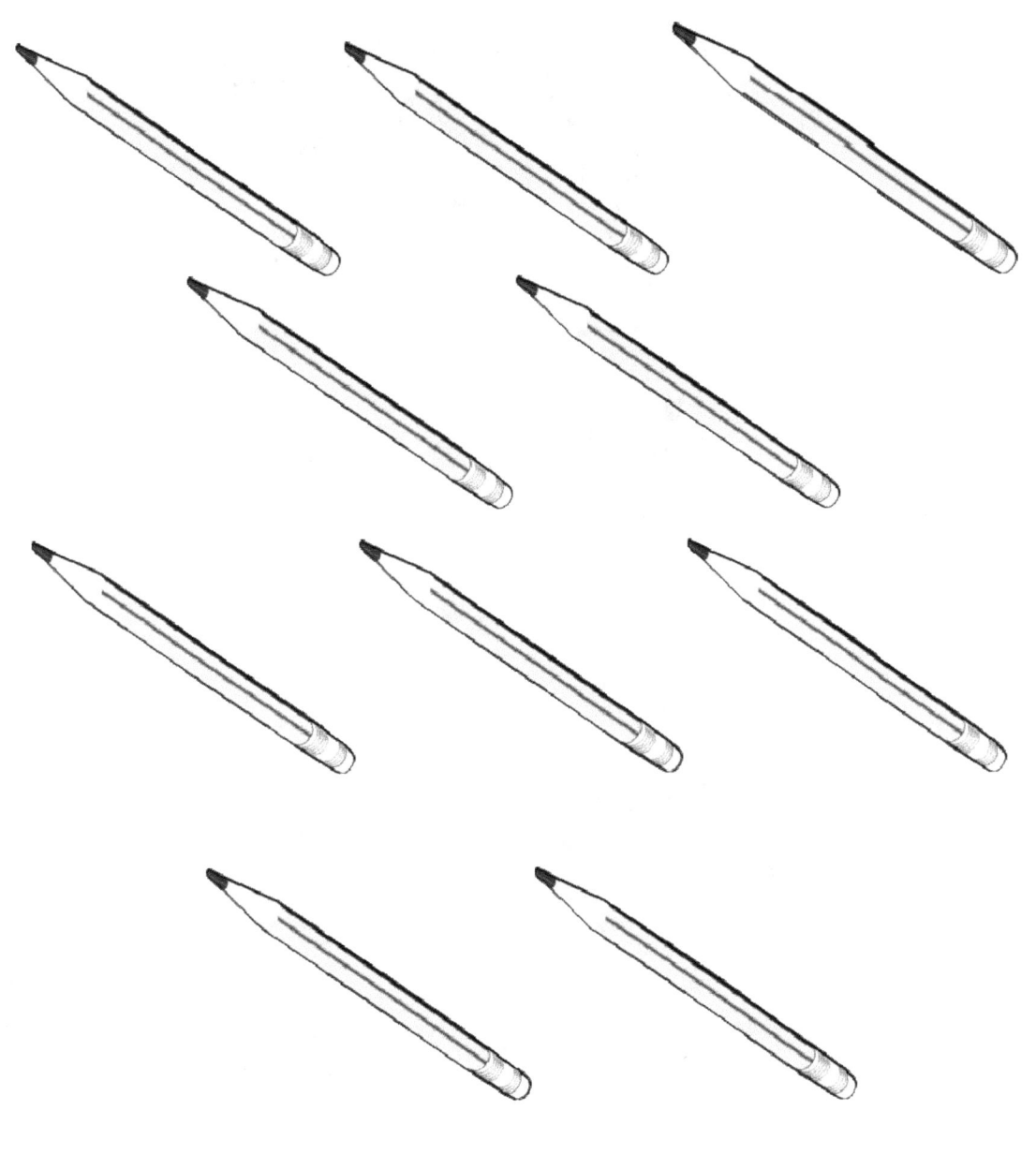

```
  80
+10 pencils
```

									90

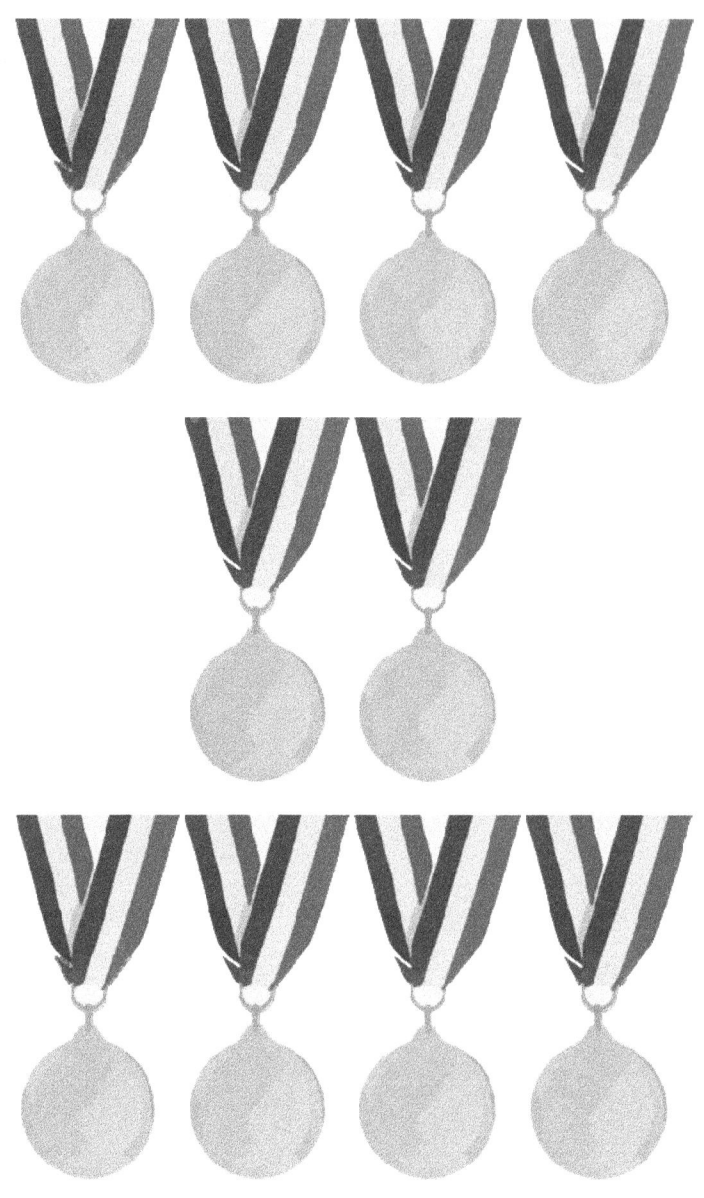

90
+10 medals

Fill in the missing numbers

									10
									20
									30
									40
									50
									60
									70
									80
									90
									100

									10
									20
									30
									40
									50
									60
									70
									80
									90
									100

Fill in the missing numbers

									10
									20
									30
									40
									50
									60
									70
									80
									90
									100

									10
									20
									30
									40
									50
									60
									70
									80
									90
									100

Label each object as **big**, **bigger**, or **biggest**

_____ _____ _____

_____ _____ _____

_____ _____ _____

Label each object as **small**, **smaller**, or **smallest**

_____ _____ _____

_____ _____ _____

_____ _____ _____

Label each object as **tall, taller,** or **tallest**

Label each object as **long, longer,** or **longest**

Position

Choose an object in each group. Name its position

1st 2nd 3rd 4th 5th

165

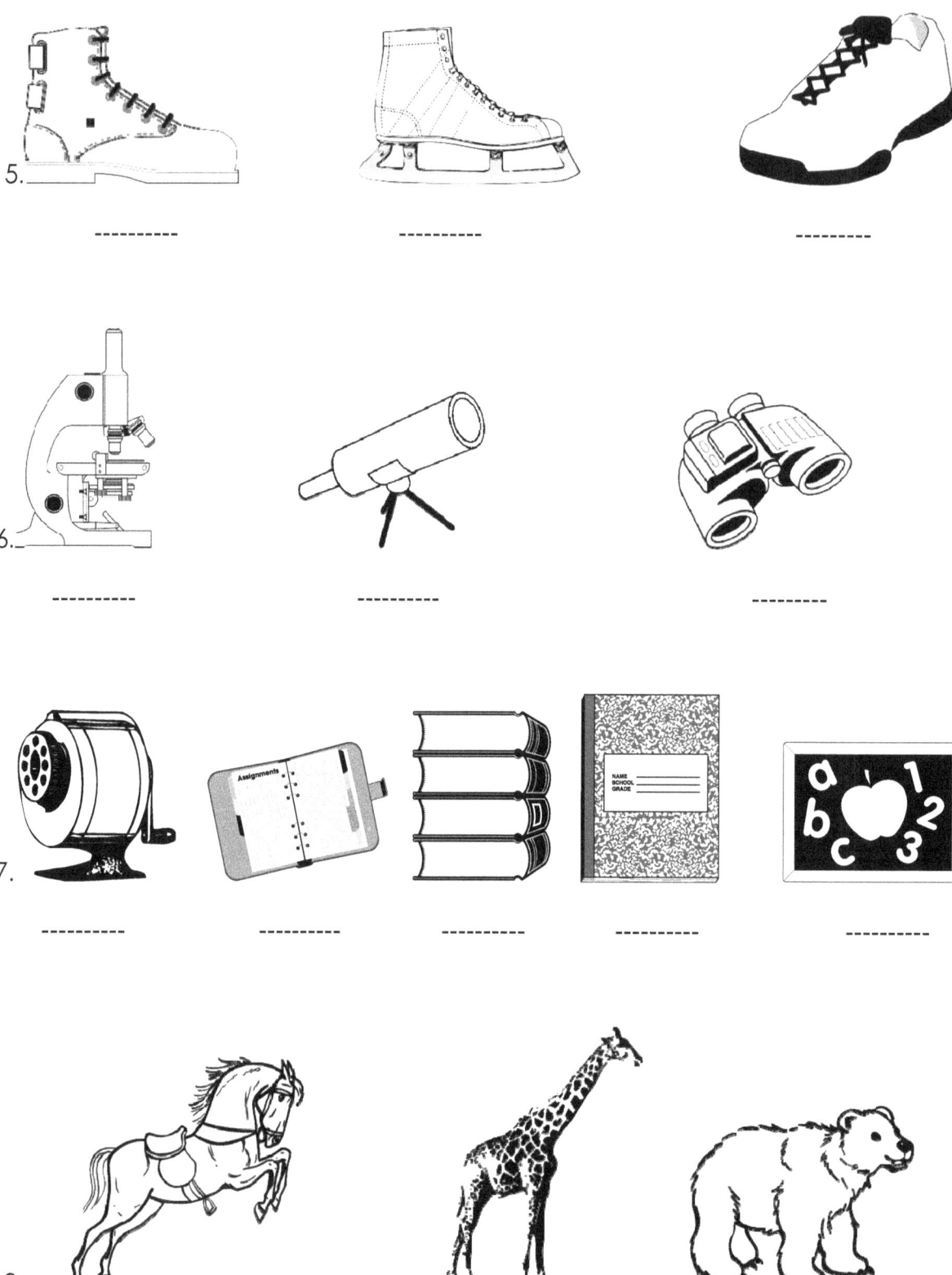

Number Lines

Use number lines for addition and subtraction

Example:

9+3=

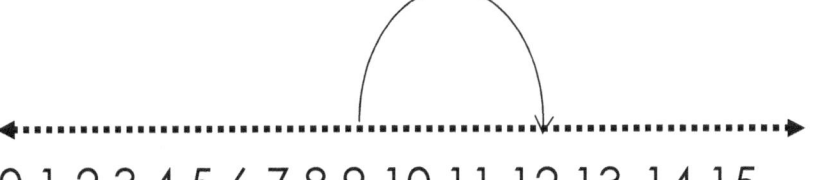

0 1 2 3 4 5 6 7 8 9 10 11 12 13 14 15

Start at number 9

Jump 3 numbers to the right (⟶)

Answer: 12

Example:

9-3=

0 1 2 3 4 5 6 7 8 9 10 11 12 13 14 15

Start at number 9

Go backwards 3 numbers to the left (⟵)

Answer: 6

Let's Practice

Use the number lines to solve each equation

12+2=

0 1 2 3 4 5 6 7 8 9 10 11 12 13 14 15 16 17 18 19 20

5+8=

0 1 2 3 4 5 6 7 8 9 10 11 12 13 14 15 16 17 18 19 20

9+9=

0 1 2 3 4 5 6 7 8 9 10 11 12 13 14 15 16 17 18 19 20

15-7 =

0 1 2 3 4 5 6 7 8 9 10 11 12 13 14 15 16 17 18 19 20

19-6=

0 1 2 3 4 5 6 7 8 9 10 11 12 13 14 15 16 17 18 19 20

10-9=

0 1 2 3 4 5 6 7 8 9 10 11 12 13 14 15 16 17 18 19 20

Graphs

Graphs can be use to get a visual understanding of both math and reading concepts.

Math example:

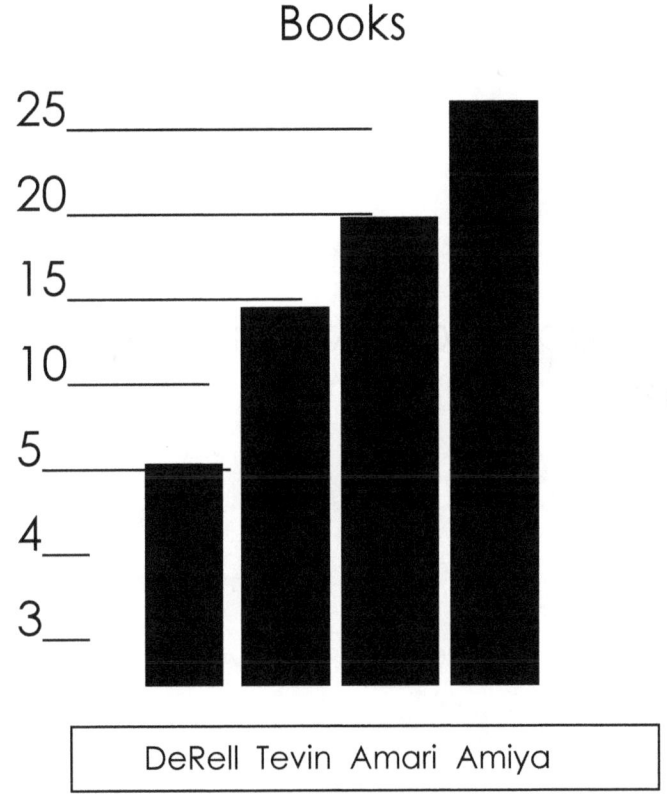

1. How many more books did Amiya read than Amari?

    Amiya   25   25
    Amari   20   - 20
                      5

2. How many books did DeRell and Tevin read all together?

    DeRell   5   5
    Tevin   15   + 15
                     20

Your turn:
1. How many more books did DeRell read than Tevin?

2. How many books did Amari and Amiya read all together?

3. How many books did Amiya and Tevin read together?

Reading example:

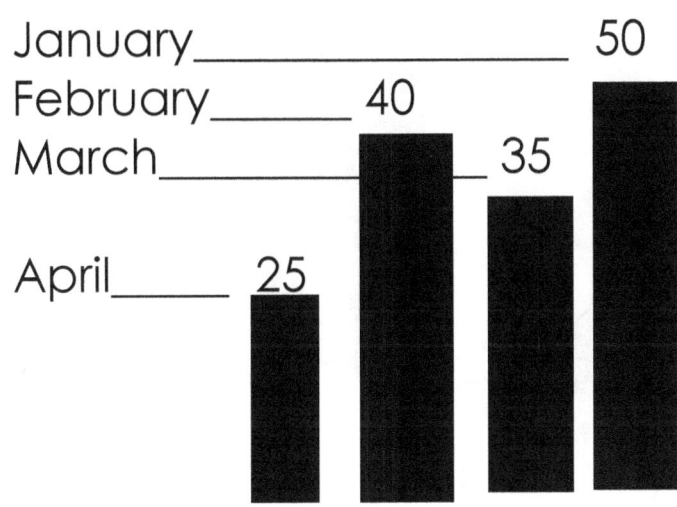

1. What is the title of the chart?

Answer:_____

2. In what month was the most books read?

Answer:_____

3. In what month was the least books read?

Answer:_____

4. How many books were read in April?

Answer:_____

Fractions
Color 1/2 of each object

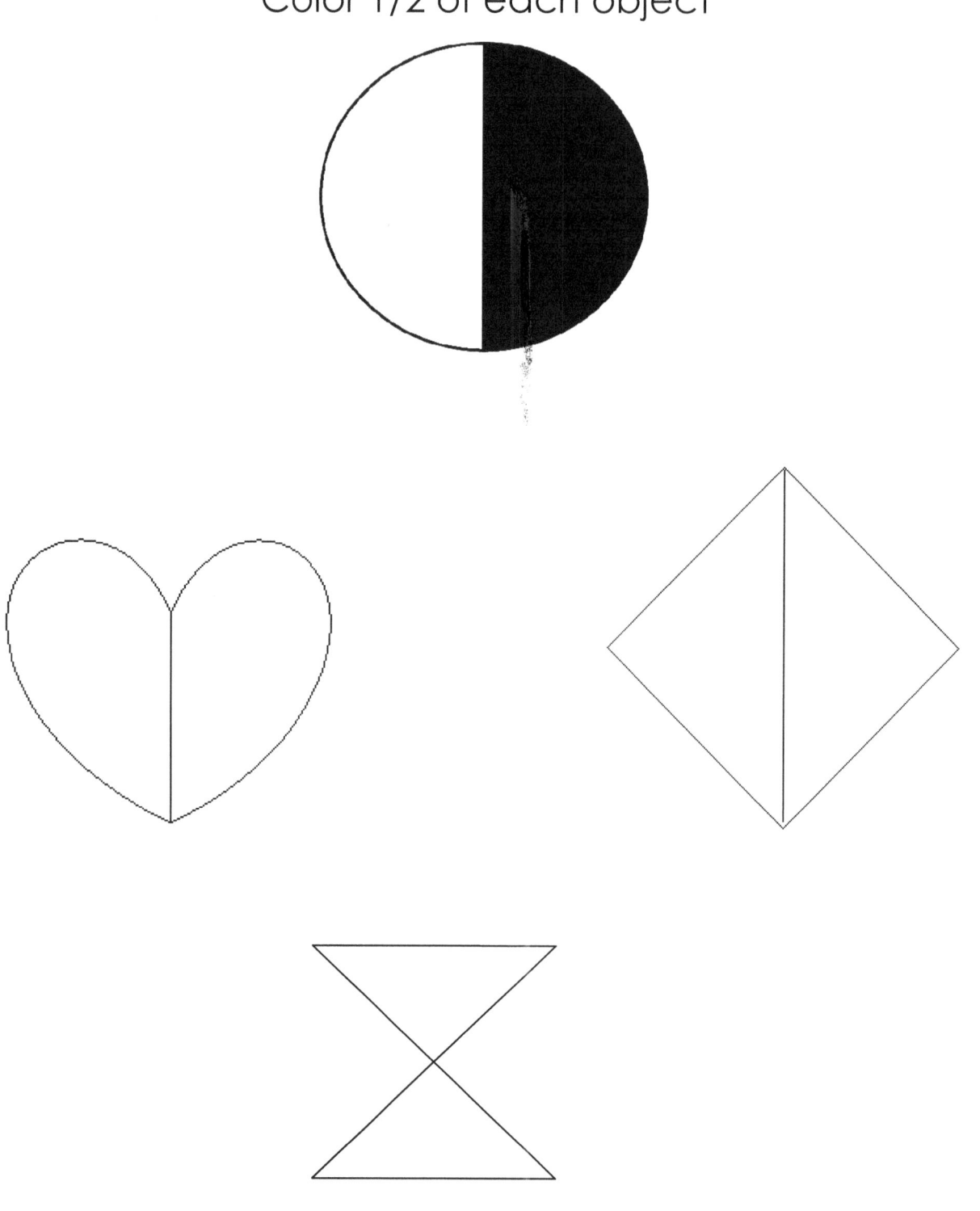

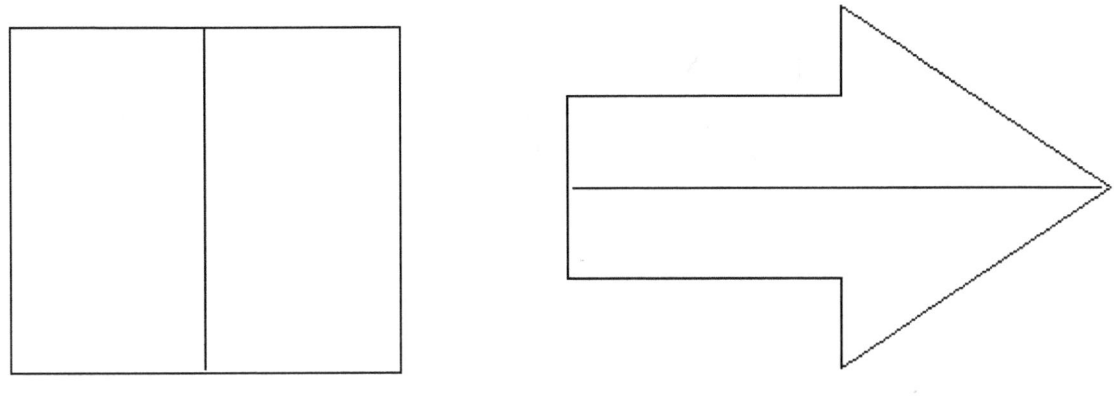
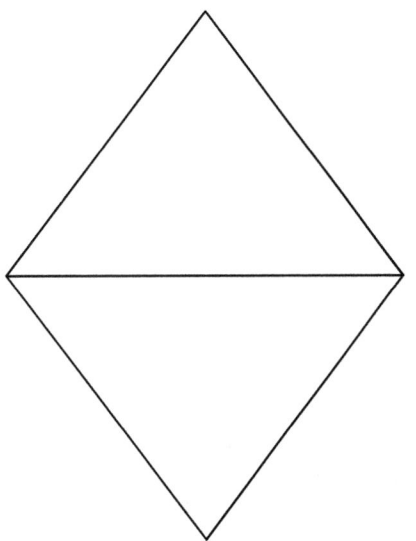

Color 1/3 of each object

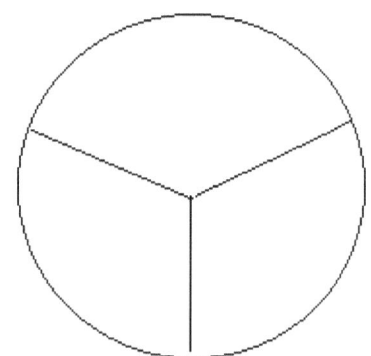

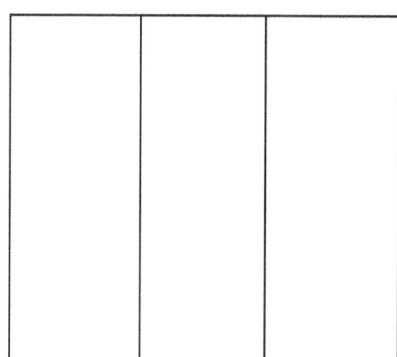

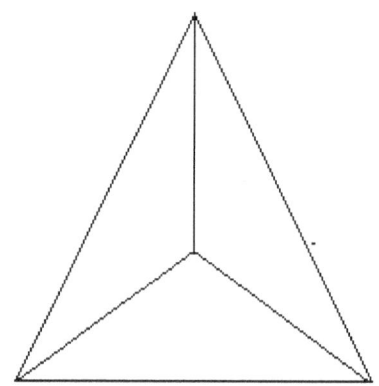

Color 1/4 of each object

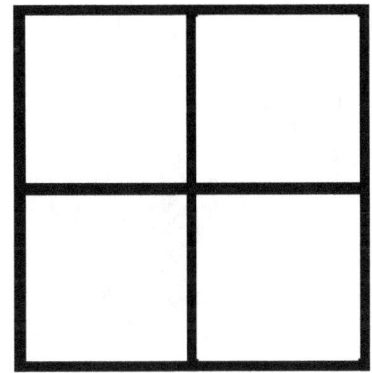 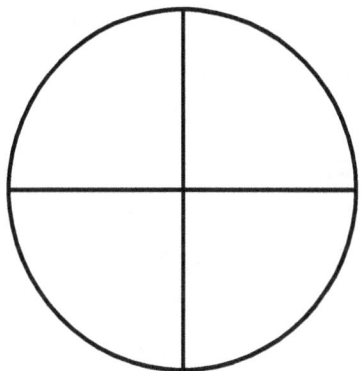

Color 2/3 of the juice boxes

Color 2/4 of the pears

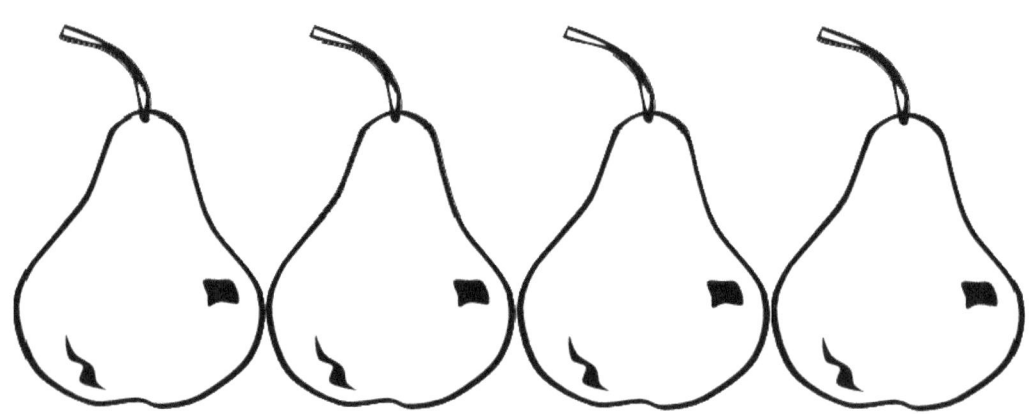

Color 3/4 of the coats

Color 1/3 of the stars

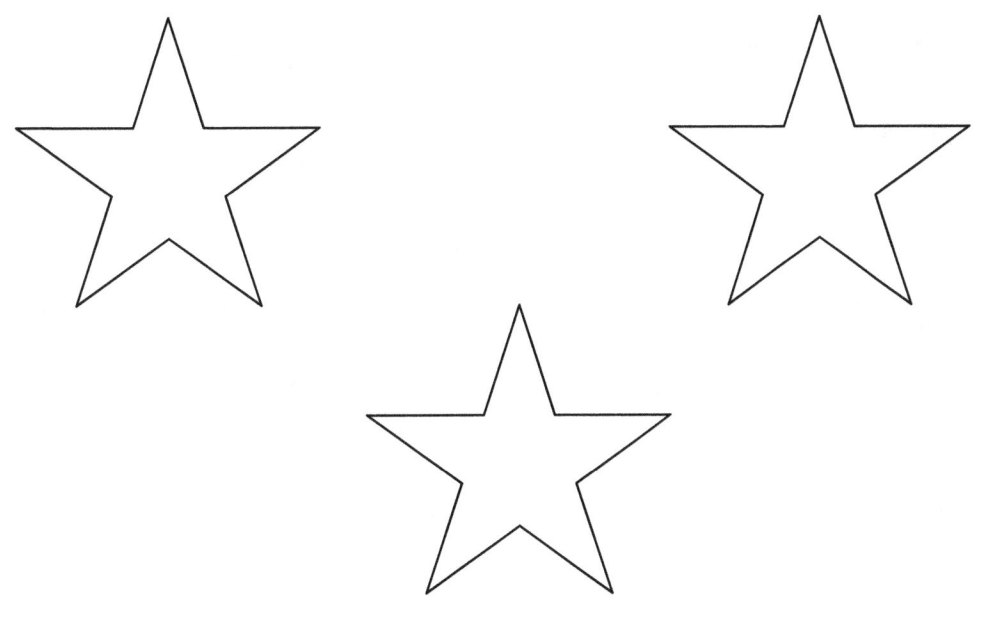

Less Than and Greater Than

Less than (<) and greater than (>) signs are used to compare numbers.

Examples:

10 > 9 reads as 10 is greater than 9 or

9 < 10 reads as 9 is less than 10

* Hint: the tip of the sign always points to the smaller number

Your turn: insert the correct sign

(1). 10　9
　　　9　10

(2). 8　13
　　　13　8

(3). 11　6
　　　6　11

(4). 5　7
　　　7　5

(5). 18　15
　　　15　18

(6). 2　5
　　　5　2

Place Value

Place Value		
Hundreds	Tens	Ones
100	10	1
1	2	8
2	8	1

The number 128 has 1 (hundred) 2 (tens) and 8 (ones).

The number 281 has 2 (hundreds) 8 (tens) and 1 (ones).

Place Value		
Hundreds	Tens	Ones
100	10	1

Write the numbers in the correct place value.

1. 234
2. 156
3. 432
4. 386
5. 521
6. 643

Place Value		
Hundreds	Tens	Ones
100	10	1

Place Value		
Hundreds	Tens	Ones
100	10	1

Introduction to Money

Money

penny
1¢   one cent

nickel
5¢   five cents

dime
10¢   ten cents

quarter
25¢   twenty-five cents

half - dollar
50¢ fifty-cents

Same As

5 pennies = 5 cents or one nickel

2 nickels = 10 cents or one dime

5 nickels = 25 cents or one quarter

Same As

2 quarters = 50 cents or one half dollar

4 quarters = $1.00 or one dollar bill

2 half dollars = $1.00 or one dollar bill

Equals $1.00

 100 pennies   20 nickels

10 dimes  4 quarters

2 half dollars

10¢ 20¢ 30¢ 40¢ 50¢

60¢ 70¢ 80¢ 90¢ $1.00

25¢ 50¢ 75¢ $1.00

50¢ $1.00

_____ _____ _____ _____ _____

_____ _____ _____ _____ _____

_____ _____ _____ _____ _____

_____ _____ _____ _____ _____

_____   _____   _____   _____   _____

   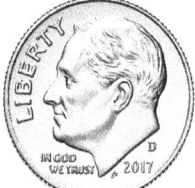 

_____   _____   _____   _____   _____

_____   _____   _____   _____

_____   _____

Health

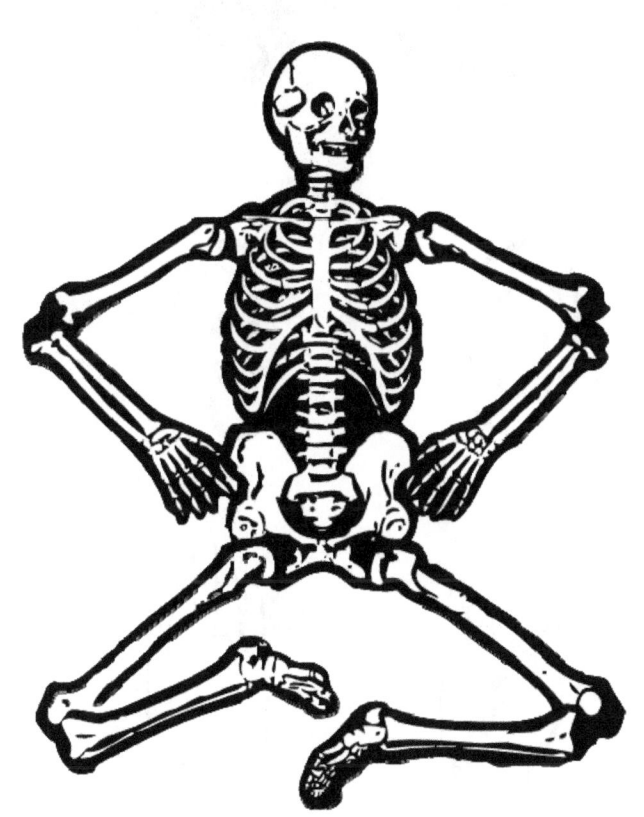

Our Five Senses

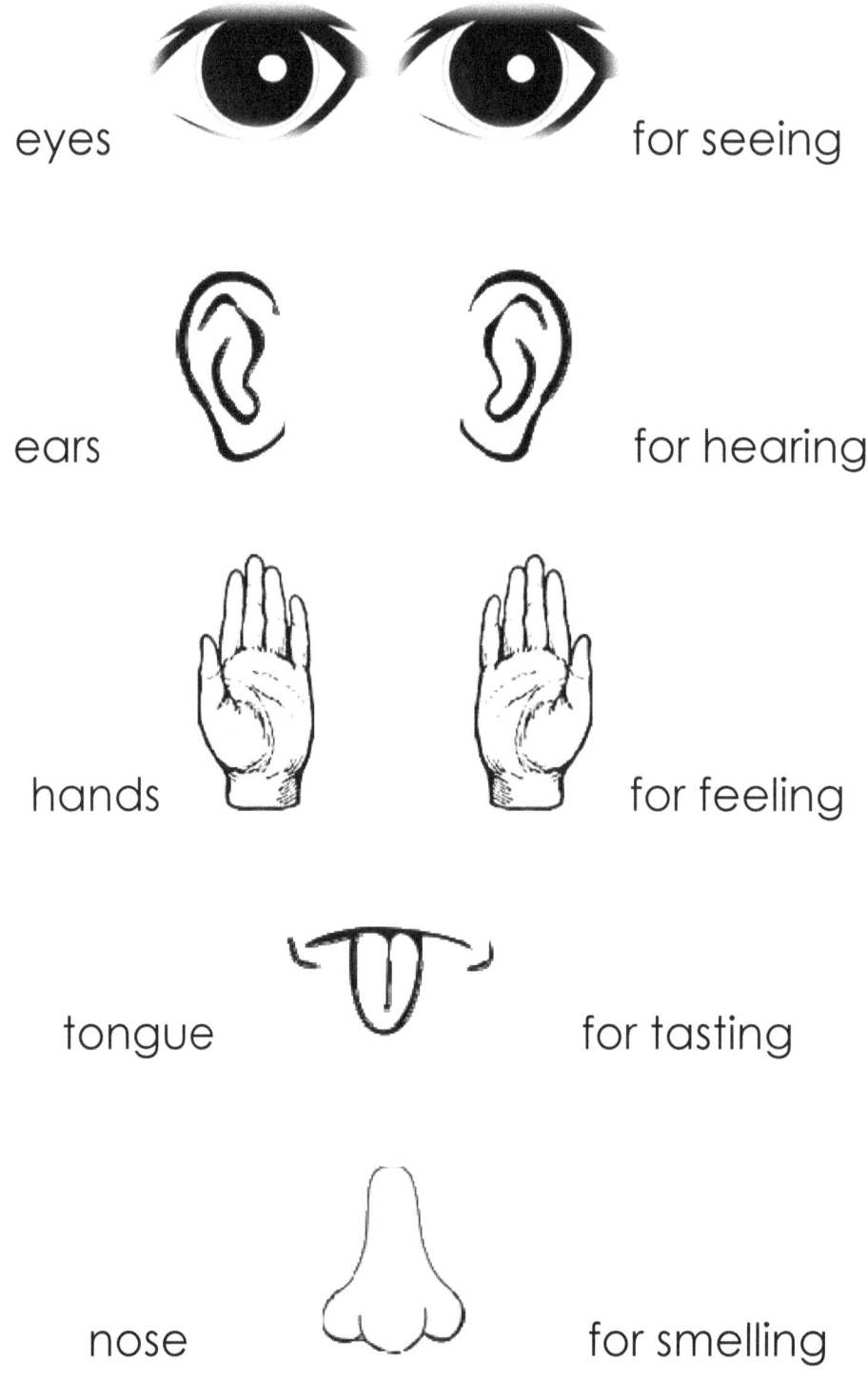

eyes — for seeing

ears — for hearing

hands — for feeling

tongue — for tasting

nose — for smelling

Parts of The Body

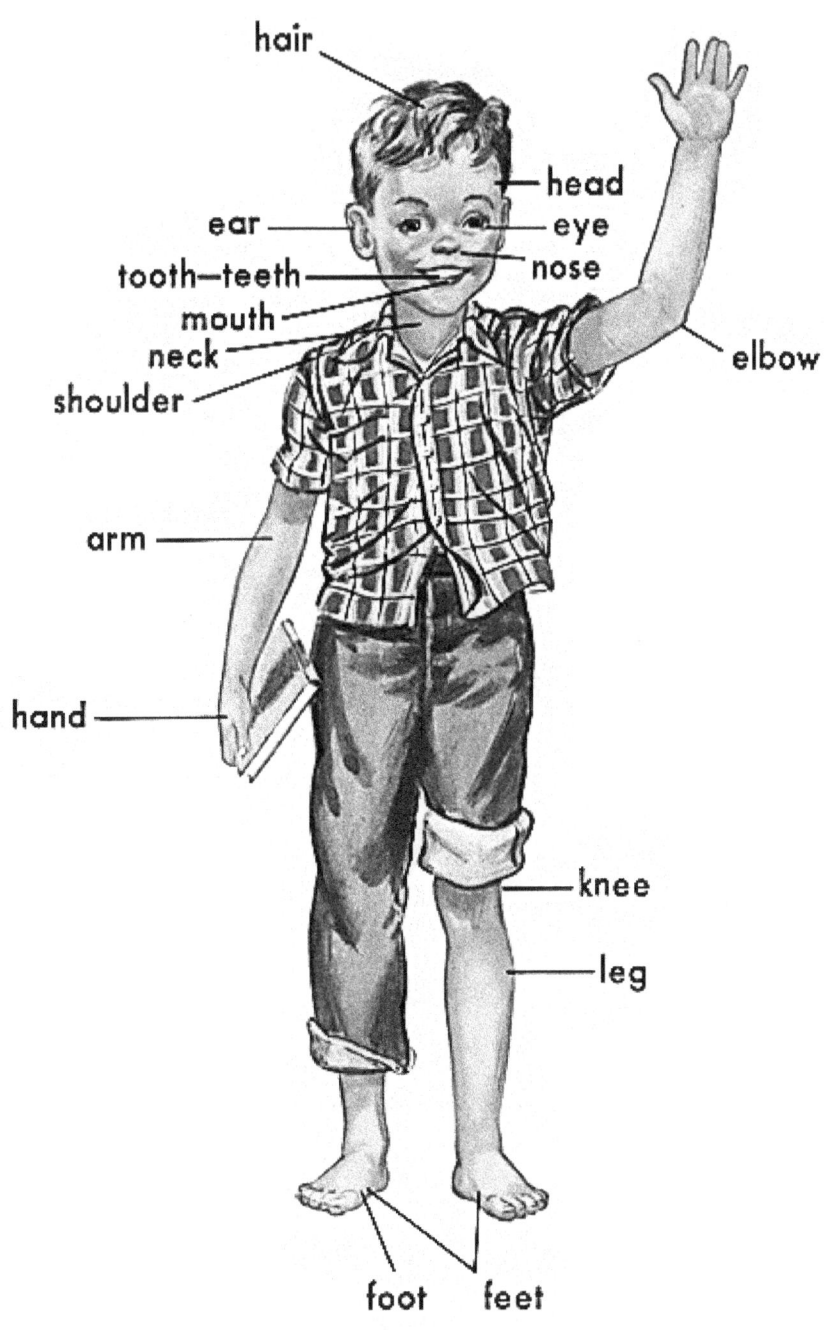

Your Turn

Label parts of the body

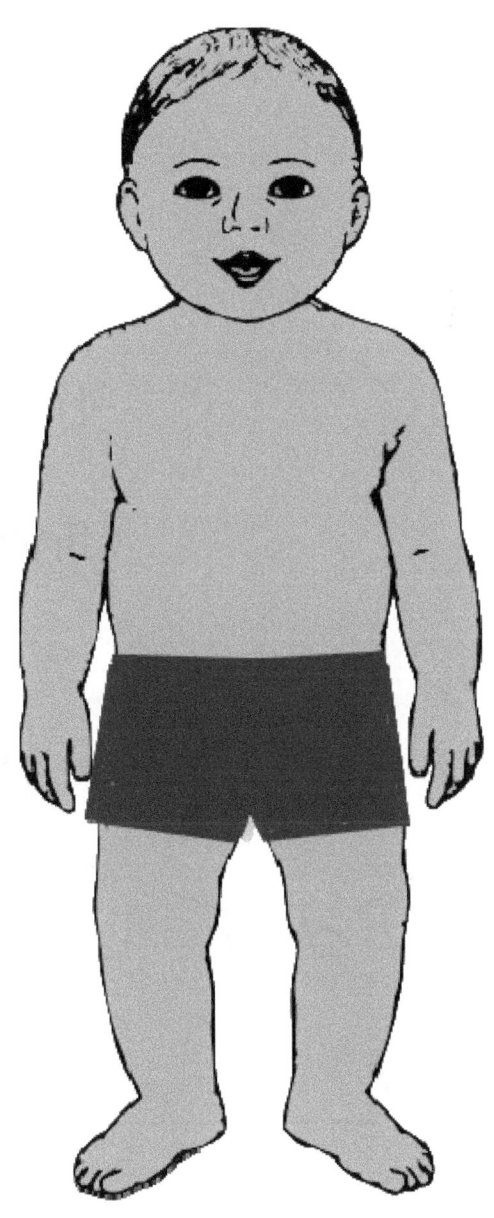

Left and Right

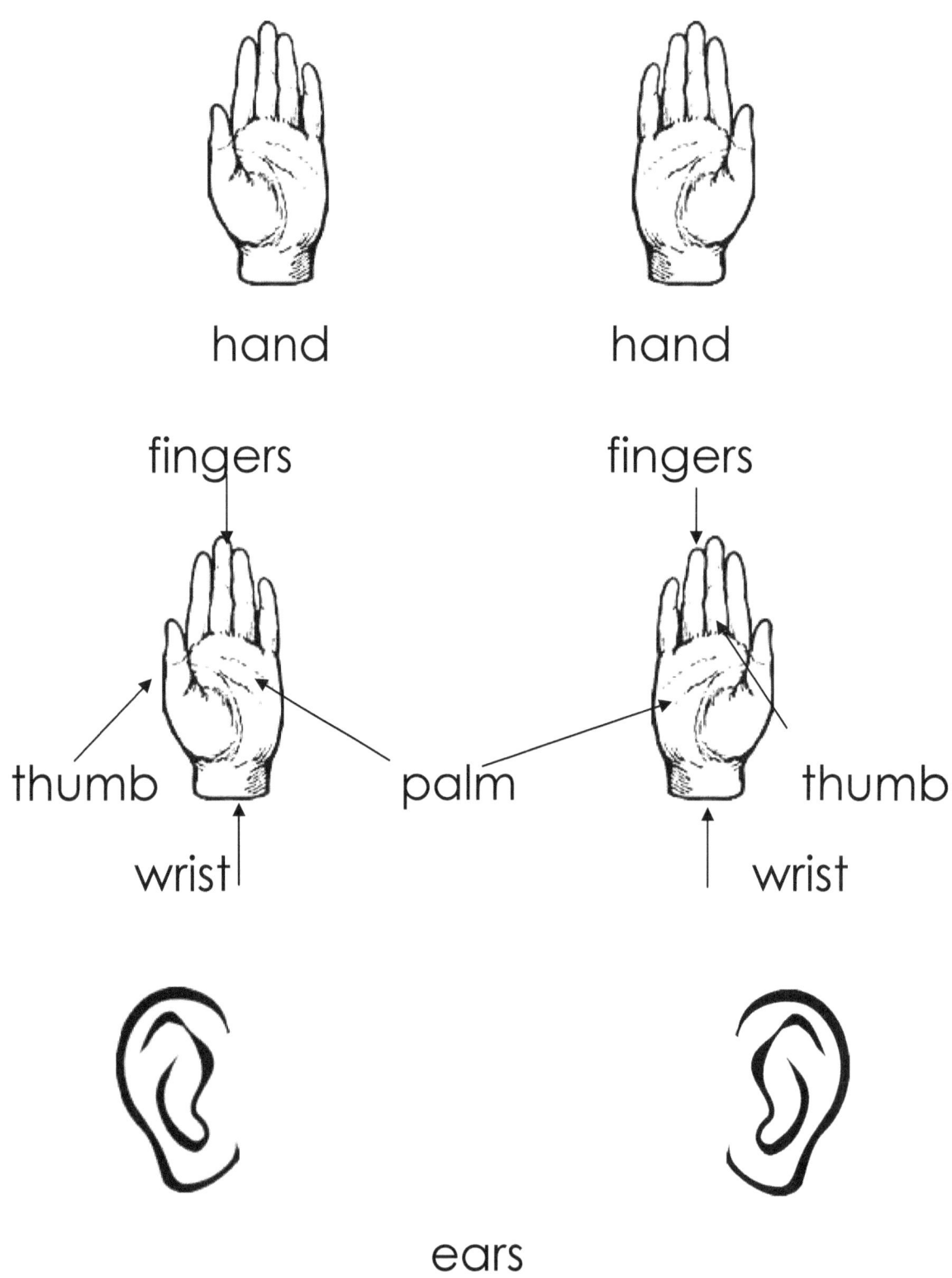

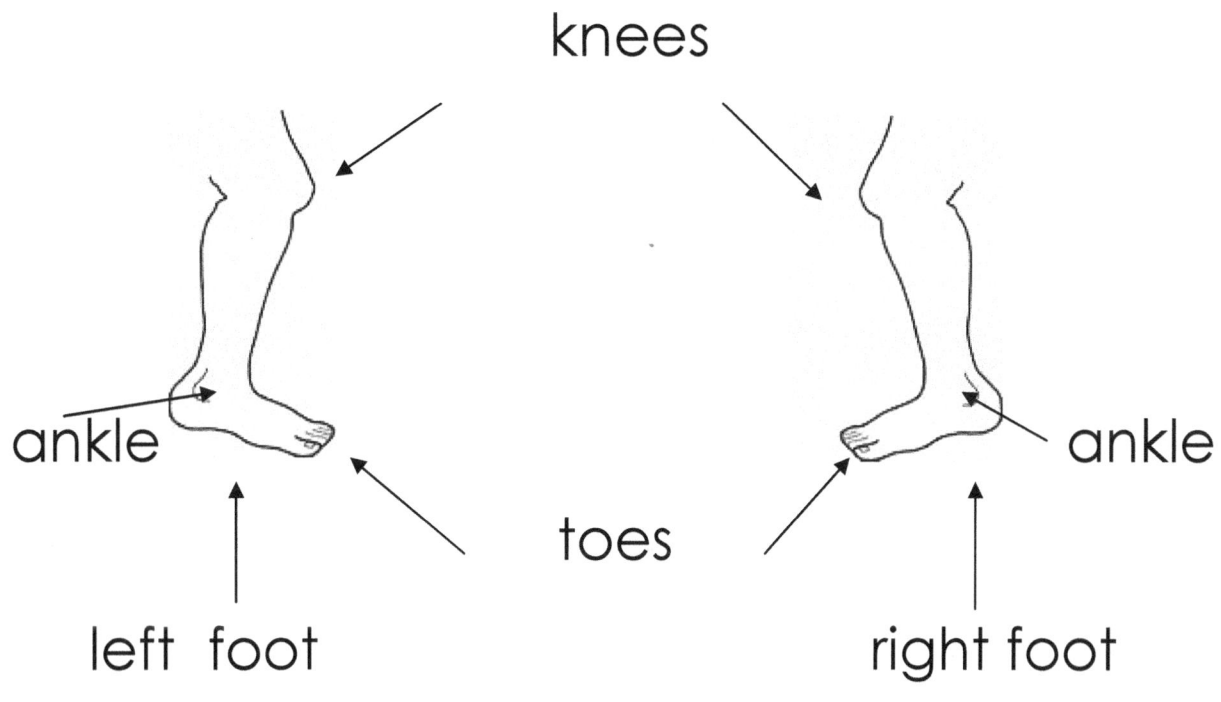

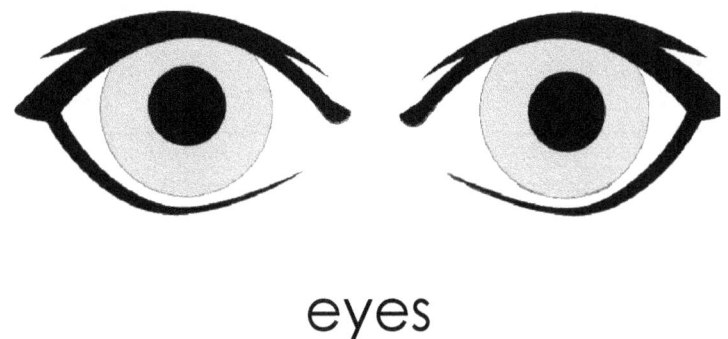

YOUR TURN

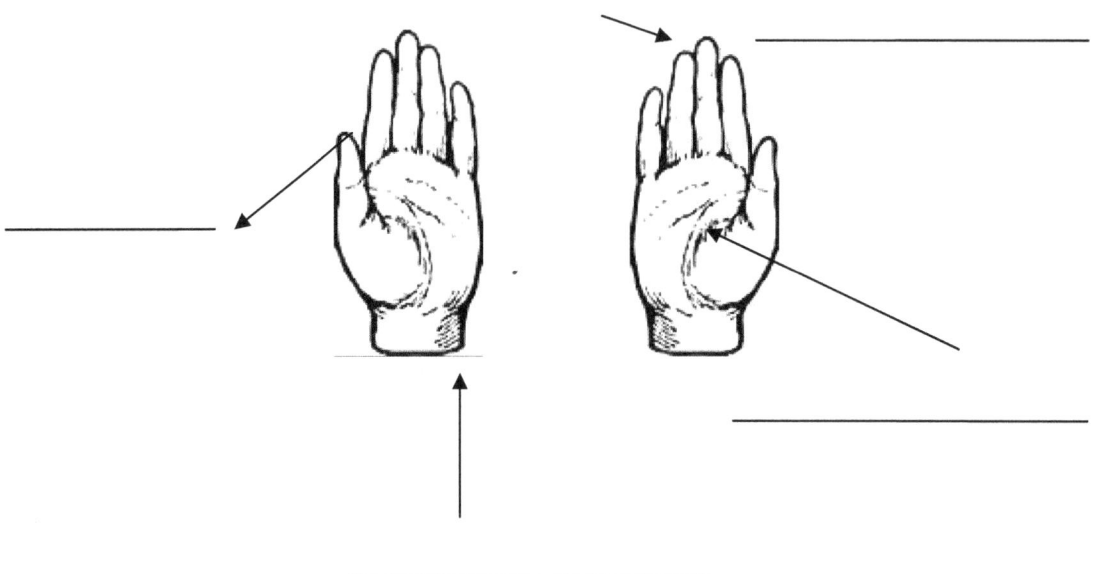

_____

_____

_____

_____

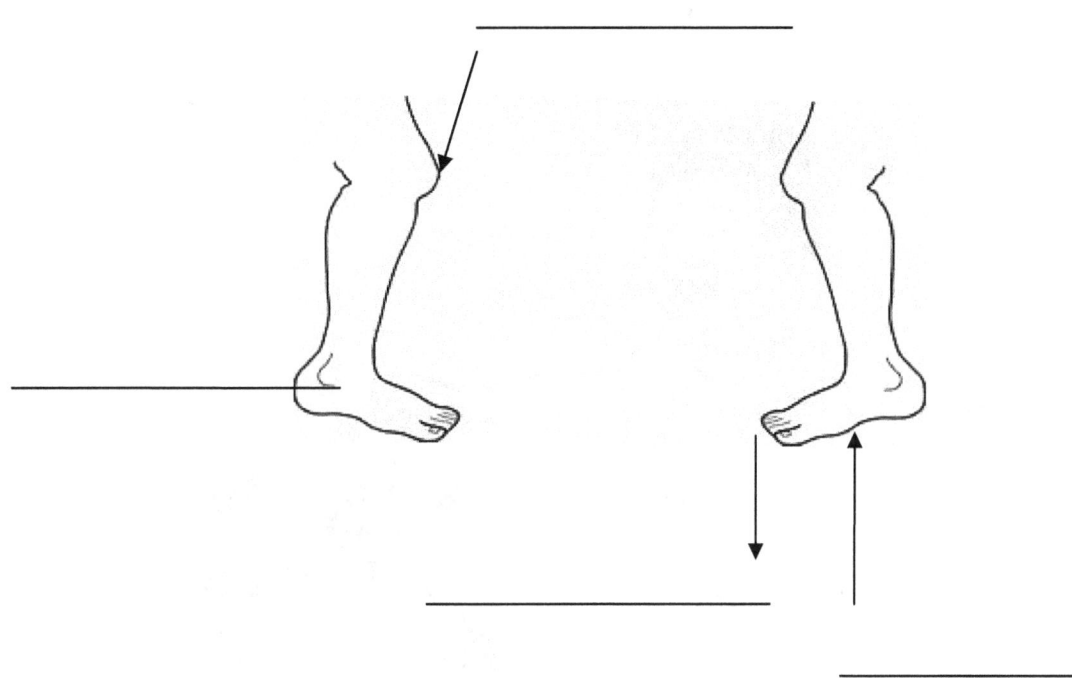

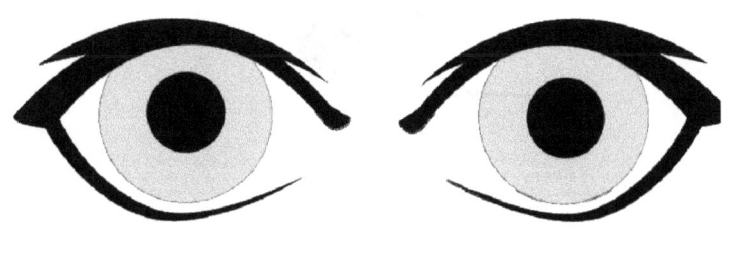

FOOD

Food is needed for growth and energy.

There are five different food groups.

Fruits

pear

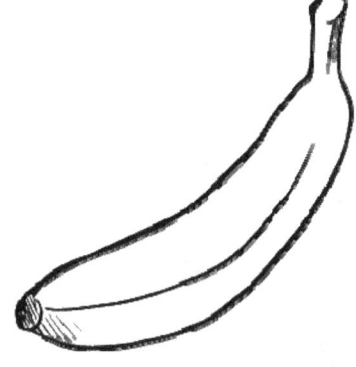
banana

watermelon

pineapple

grapes

Vegetables

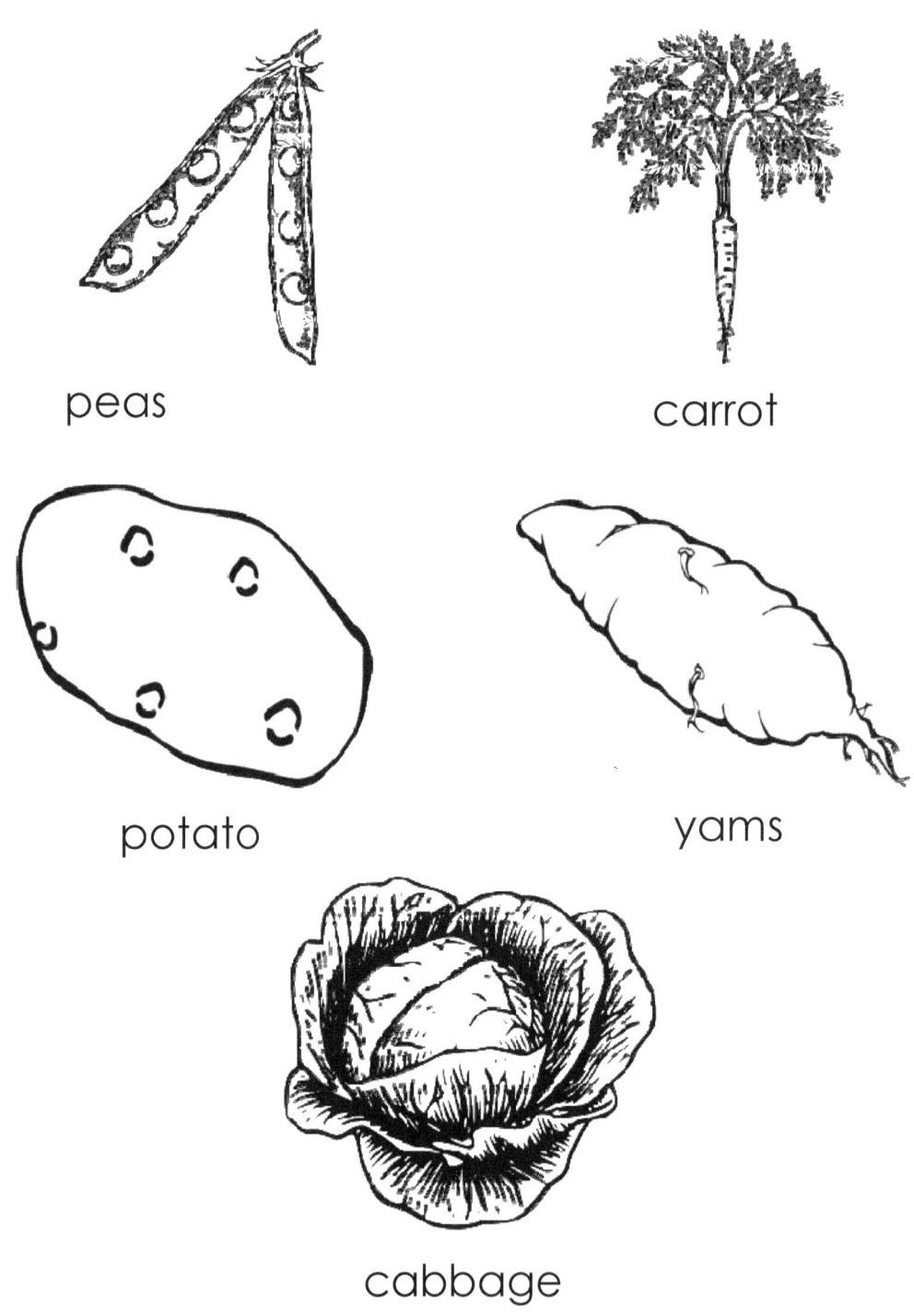

peas

carrot

potato

yams

cabbage

Proteins

fish

turkey

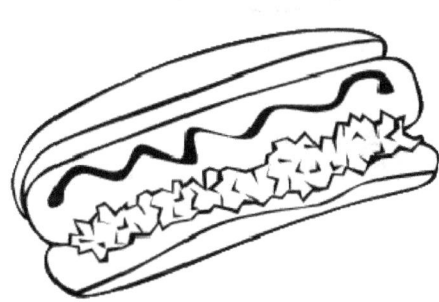
hotdog

chicken

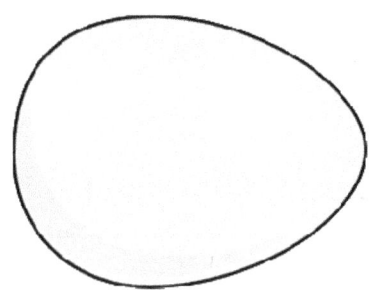
egg

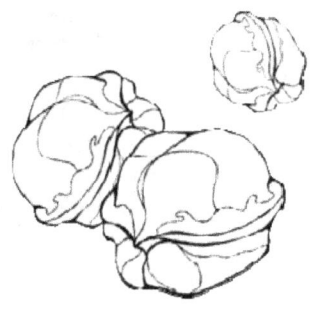
walnuts

Dairy

milk

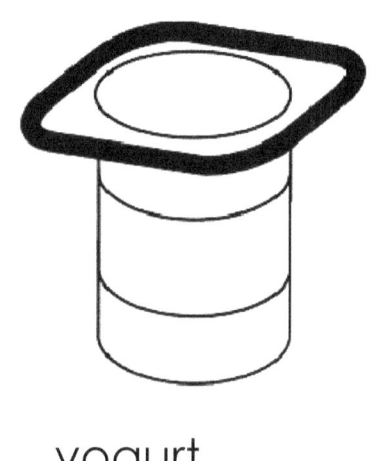
yogurt

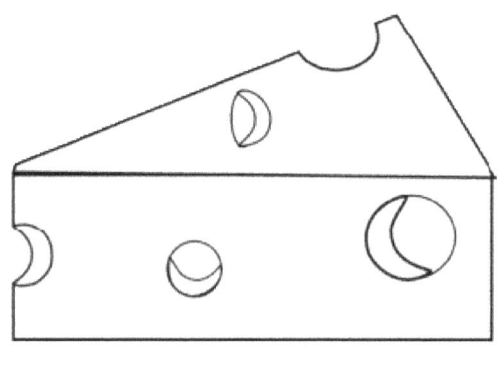
cheese

Grains

rolls

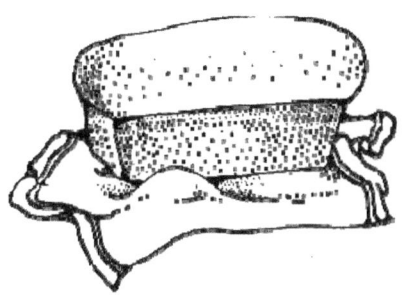
bread

cereal

pizza

wheat crackers

Water

Drinking water keeps our bodies alive and hydrated. Plants also need water to grow.

Earth Science

Clouds

Tiny droplets or frozen crystals of water

Earth

Third planet from the sun

Supports life

Is not a perfect circle

Lightning

Electricity made from a thunderstorm

Thunder is a sound wave caused by lightning

Moon

Rotates around the earth

Can be seen during the day

Mostly seen at night

Rainbow

Forms when the sunlight and rain comes together

A circle of various colors but view as an arch

Raindrops

Water that falls as drops from clouds

Snow

White flakes of ice that falls from the sky

Solar System

The sun and all of the planets that rotates around it

Star

A large bright sphere of hot gas

Seen in the sky at night

Sun

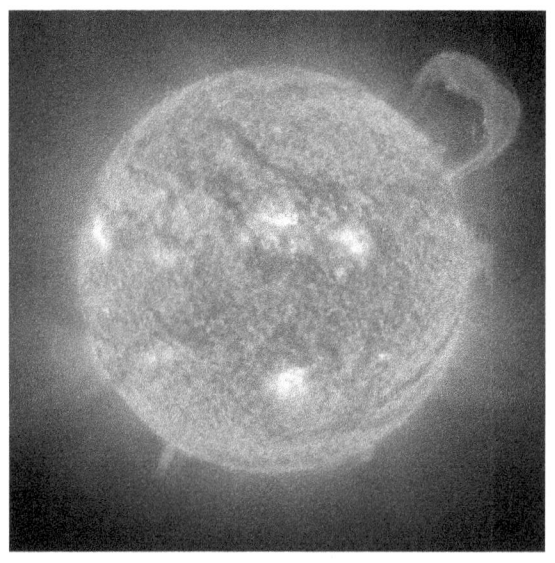

Star located in the middle (center) of the solar system

The brightest star in the sky

Supplies energy for life on earth

Flower Parts

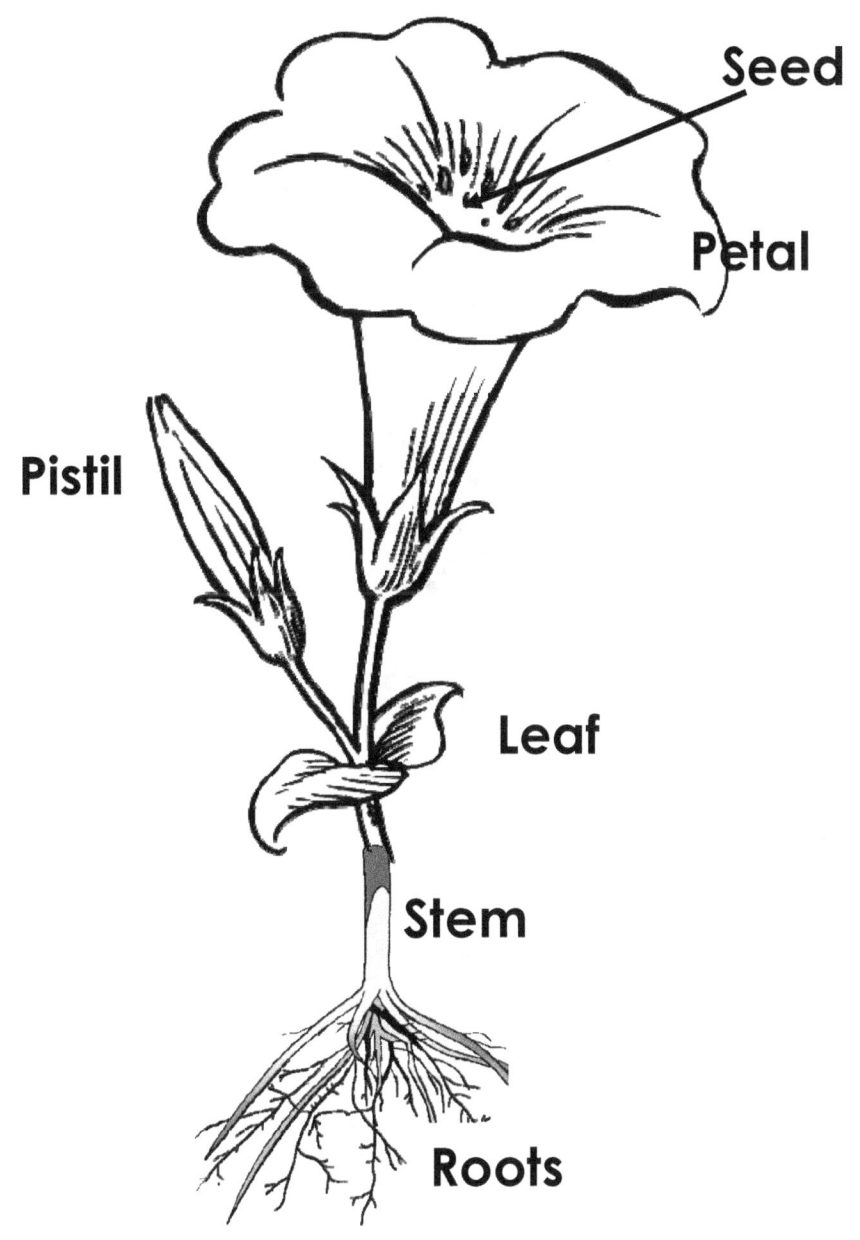

Your Turn

Tree Parts

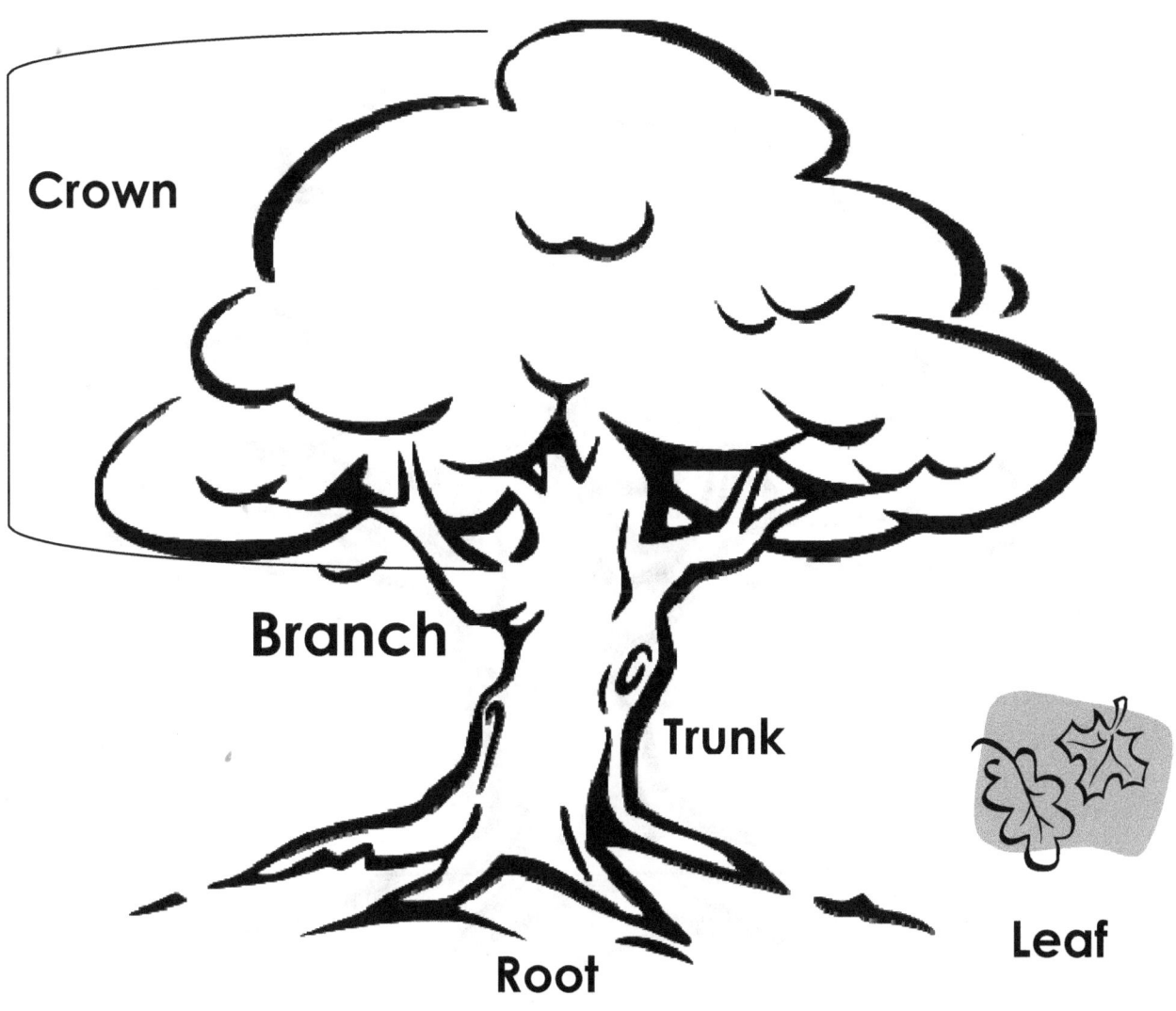

Your Turn

Time

Did you know?

There are 365 days in a year but 366 in a leap year.

A leap year comes every 4 years.

A year has 12 months:

1. January
2. February
3. March
4. April
5. May
6. June
7. July
8. August
9. September
10. October
11. November
12. December

A month has 30 or 31 days: There are 30 days in September, April, June, and November.

There are 31 days in January, March, May, July, August, October, and December.

February has 28 days but 29 days in each leap year.

A month has an average of 4 weeks. Each week has 7 days.

1. Sunday (Sun.)
2. Monday (Mon.)
3. Tuesday (Tues.)
4. Wednesday (Wed.)
5. Thursday (Thurs.)
6. Friday (Fri.)
7. Saturday (Sat.)

The 12 months are divided into 4 seasons:

- Spring: March April May
- Summer: June July August
- Autumn: September October November
- Winter: December January February

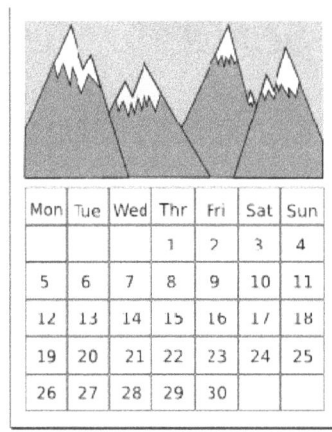

Your Turn

Did you know?

There are ____ days in a year but _____ in a leap year. A leap year comes every ___ years.

A year has ____ months:

1. _____
2. _____
3. _____
4. _____
5. _____
6. _____
7. _____
8. _____
9. _____
10. _____
11. _____
12. _____

A month has ___ or ____ days. There are _____ days in September, April, June, and November.

There are ___ days in January, March, May, July, August, October, and December.

February has ___ days but ___ days in each leap year.

A month has an average of ____ weeks. Each week has ___ days.

1. _____
2. _____
3. _____
4. _____
5. _____
6. _____
7. _____

The 12 months are divided into _____ seasons

Spring: _____ _____ _____

Summer: _____ _____ _____

Autumn: _____ _____ _____

Winter: _____ _____ _____

Telling Time

Did you know?

60 seconds is the same as 1 minute

60 minutes is the same as 1 hour

There are 24 hours in a day

A clock has hands:

  The short hand points to the hour

  The long hand points to the minutes

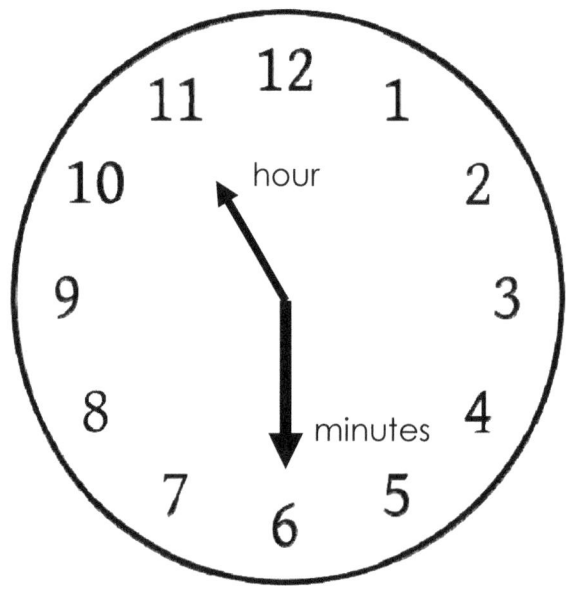

11:30

By The Hour

12:00 o'clock

Half Past

7:30

Your Turn

Your Turn

Review Time

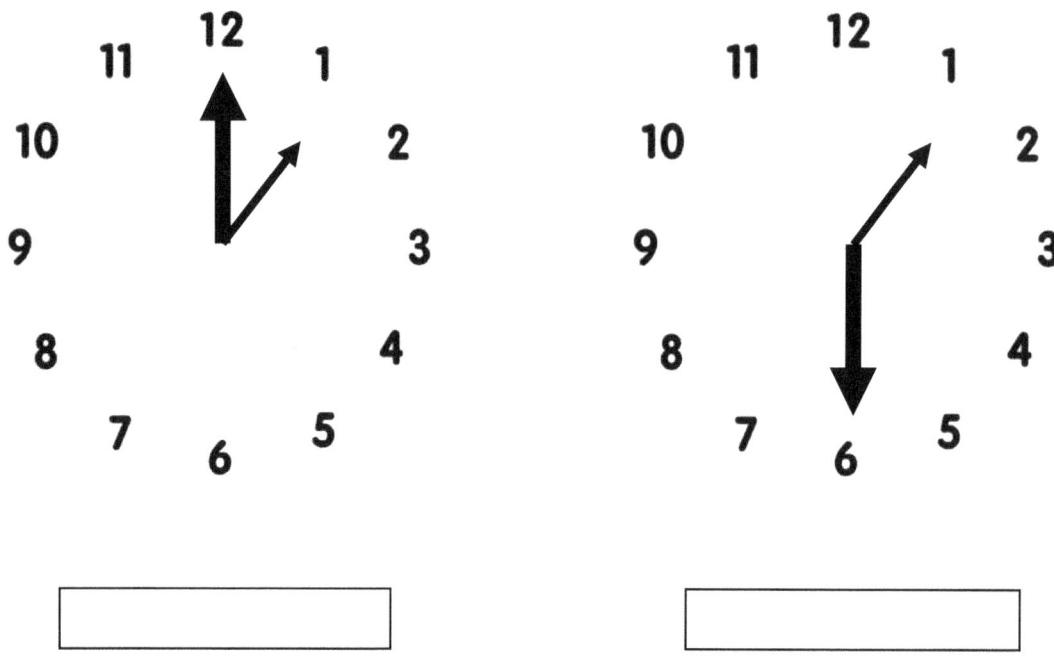

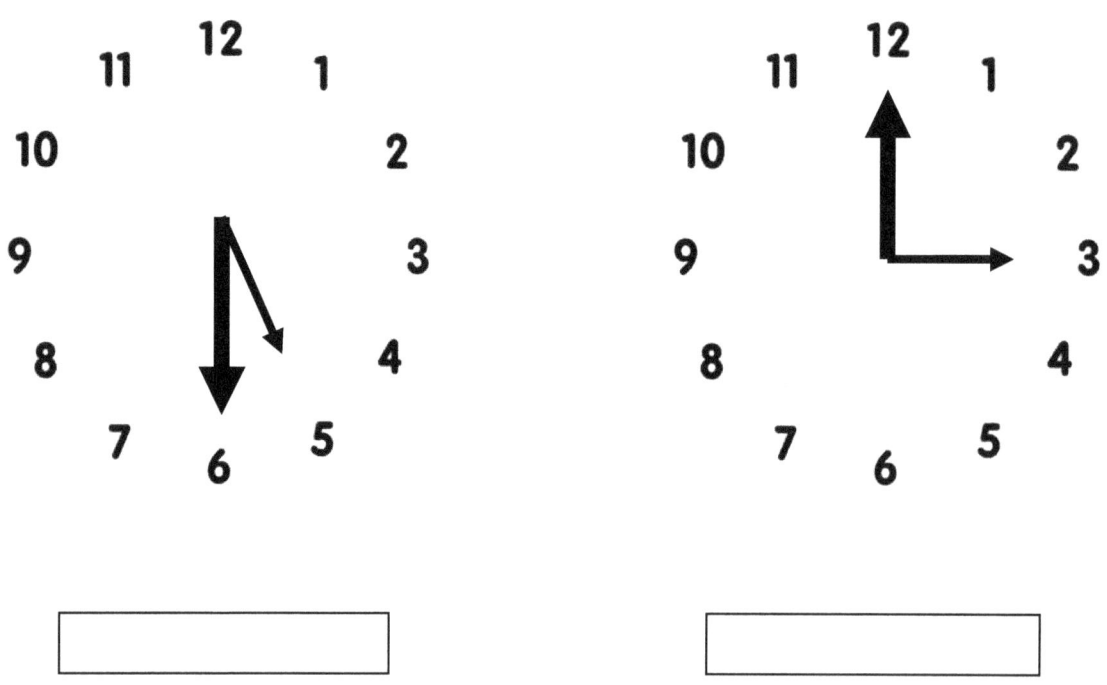

ADVANCE TIME TELLING

11:15 or
Quarter past 11

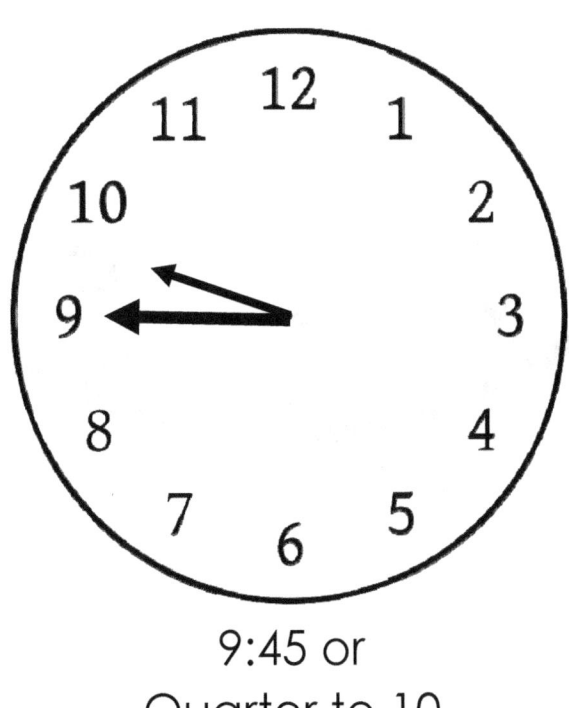

9:45 or
Quarter to 10

Use the clocks to practice telling time

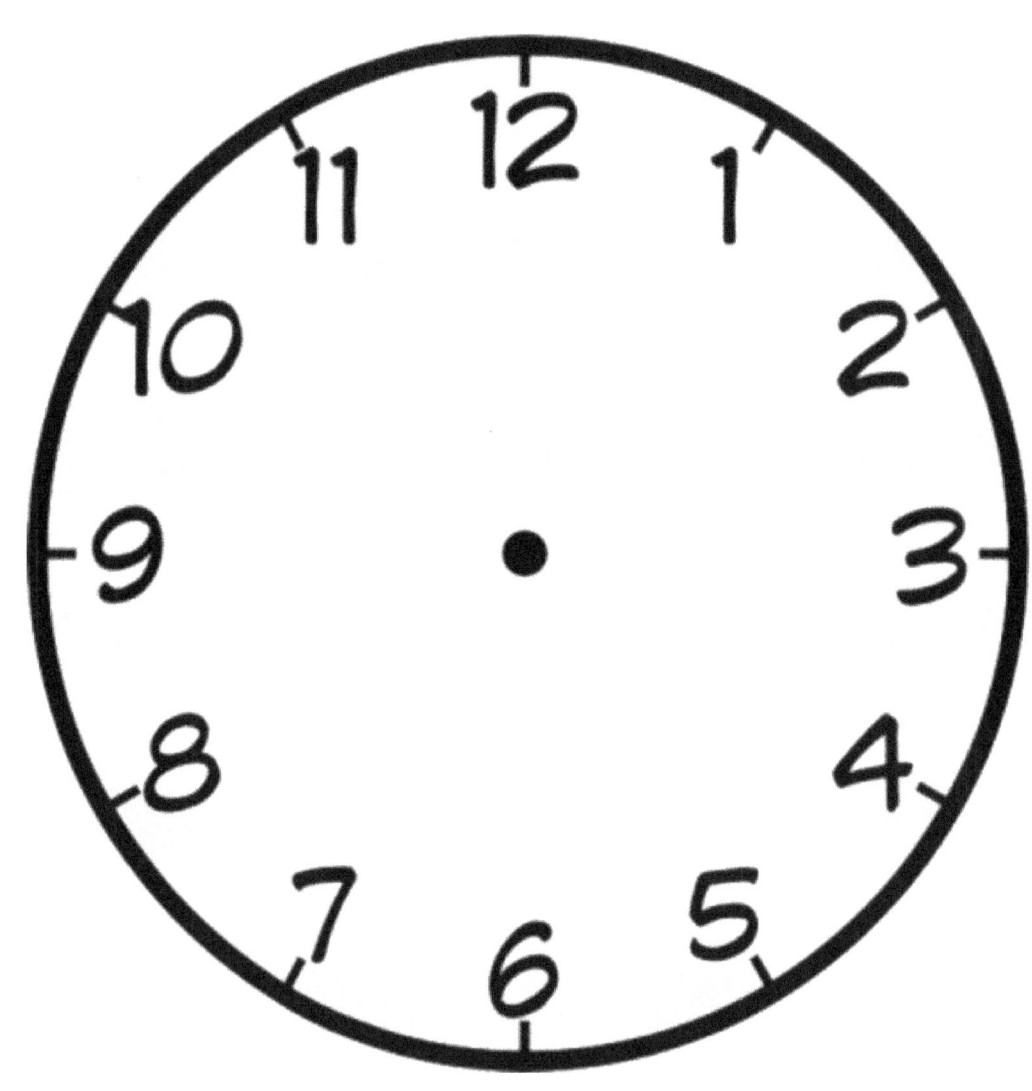

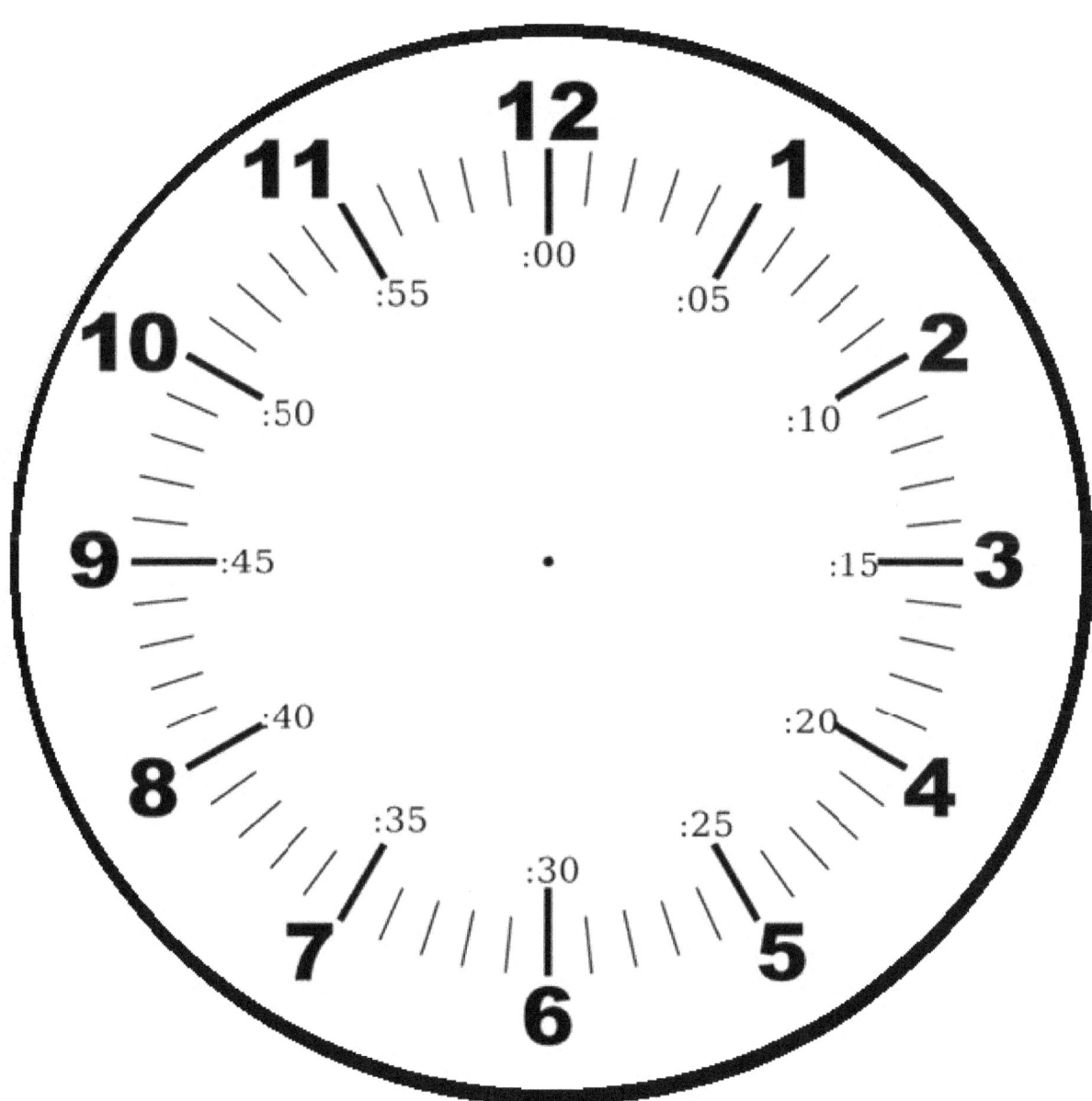

PRACTICE TIME

Cut out the hands to practice telling time on the clocks

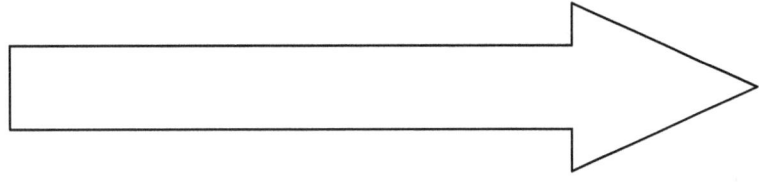

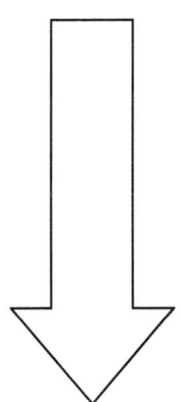

Musical

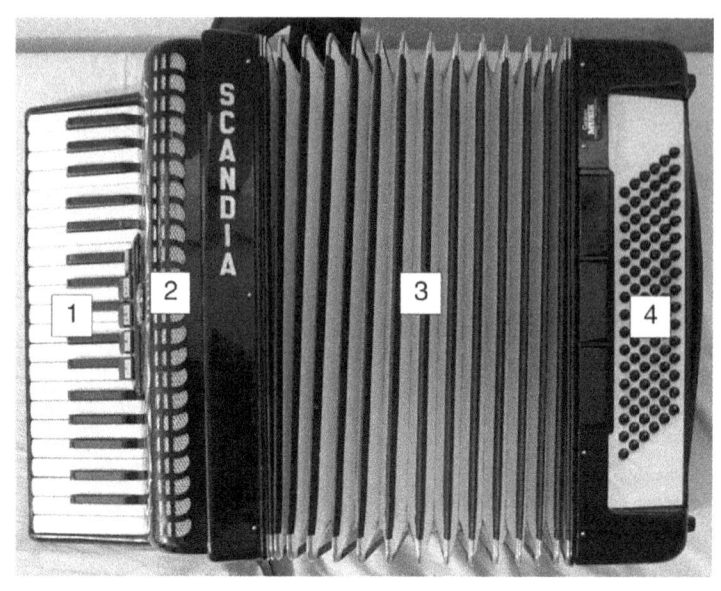

Accordion

Banjo

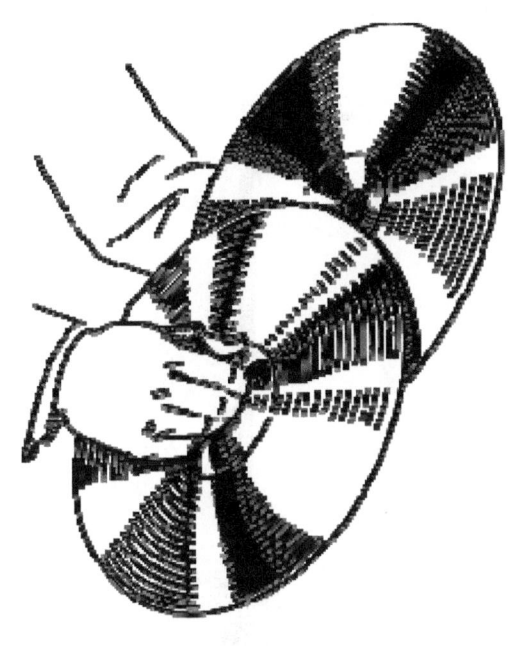

Cymbals

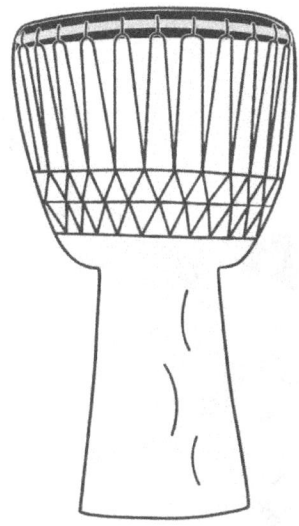

Djembe African Drums

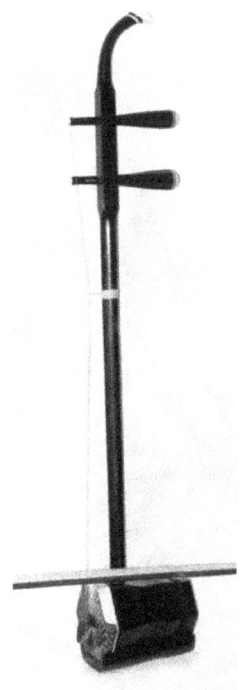

Erhu

Guitar

Harmonica

Harp

Lyre

Musical Bow

Notes

Saxophone

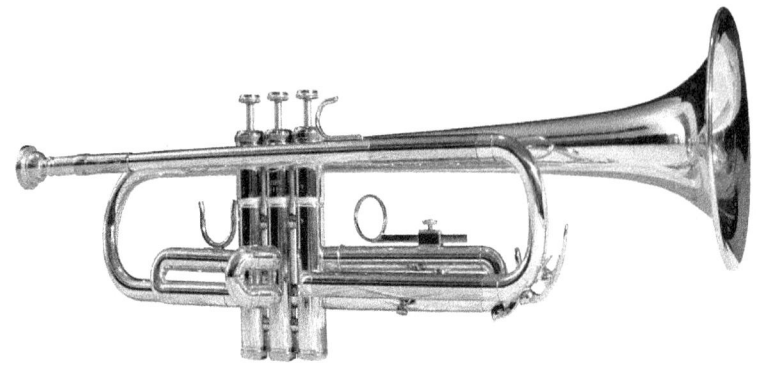

Trumpet

Ukulele

Violin

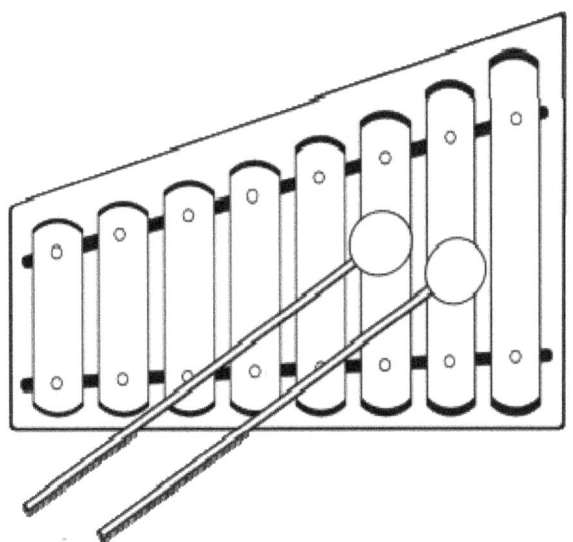

Xylophone

Did you know?

Instruments are grouped in "musical families".

The families are based on how the instruments are played and the sounds that they make:

1. String-plucked, bow or struck; example (violin)
2. Brass-blown into but are made of brass; example (trumpet)
3. Percussions – hit; example (drums)
4. Wood winds-air is blown into mouth piece; example (flute)

Transportation Then and Now

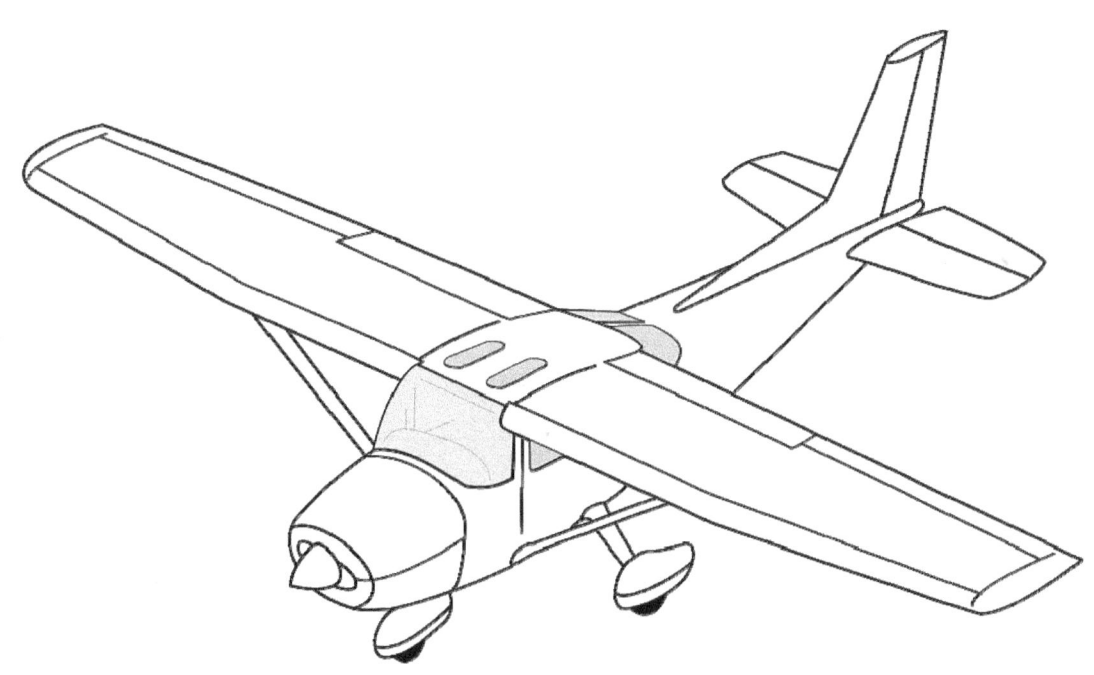

HIBERNIA STEAM FIRE ENGINE AND HORSES

History

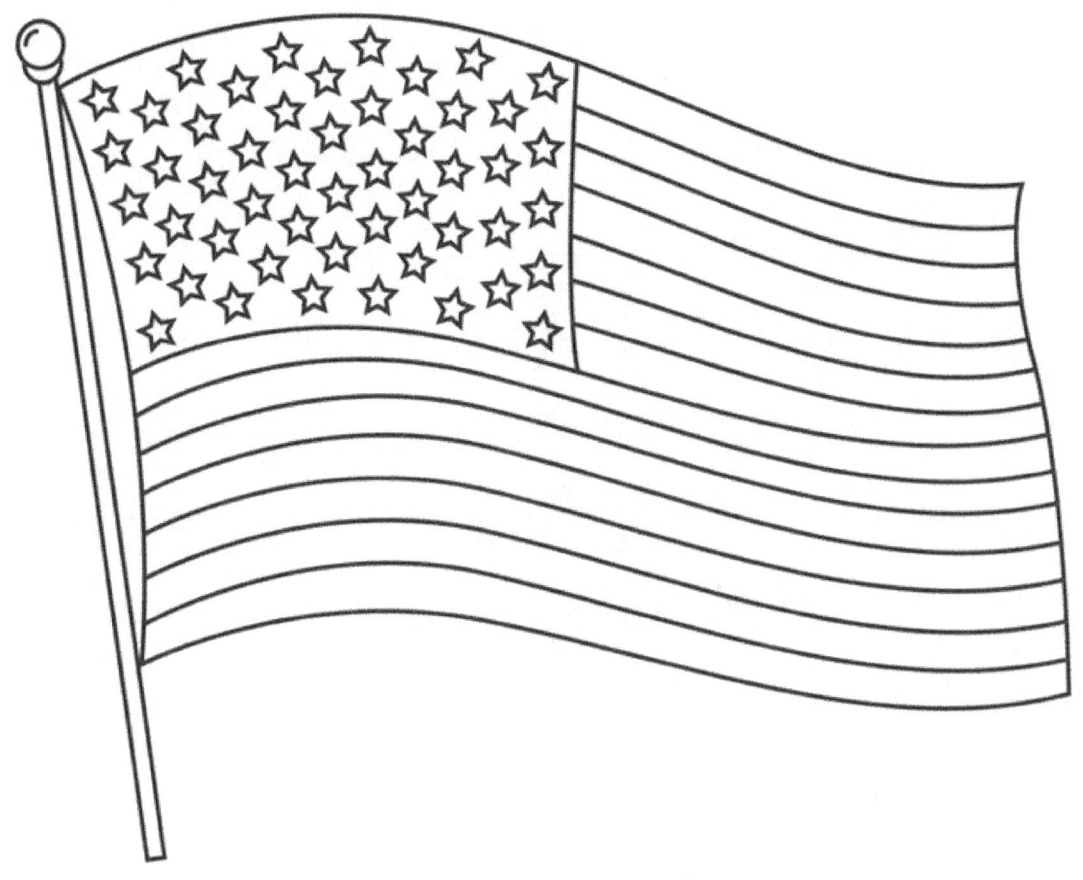

I Pledge Allegiance

"I pledge allegiance to the Flag of the United States of America, and to the Republic for which it stands, one Nation under God, indivisible, with liberty and justice for all."

Did you know The American Bald Eagle

- Was adopted as the national bird symbol in 1782?
- Scientific name is "Haliaeetus Leucocephalus" ?
- Wingspan can grow up to 7 feet?
- Can fly up to 30 miles per hour?
- Can dive at100 miles per hour?

America The Beautiful

Alabama	Louisiana	Ohio
Alaska	Maine	Oklahoma
Arizona	Maryland	Oregon
Arkansas	Massachusetts	Pennsylvania
California	Michigan	Rhode Island
Colorado	Minnesota	South Carolina
Connecticut	Mississippi	South Dakota
Delaware	Missouri	Tennessee
Florida	Montana	Texas
Georgia	Nebraska	Utah
Hawaii	Nevada	Vermont
Idaho	New Hampshire	Virginia
Illinois	New Jersey	Washington
Indiana	New Mexico	West Virginia
Iowa	New York	Wisconsin
Kansas	North Carolina	Wyoming
Kentucky	North Dakota	

THE UNITED STATES OF AMERICA

THE UNITED STATES OF AMERICA

Alabama

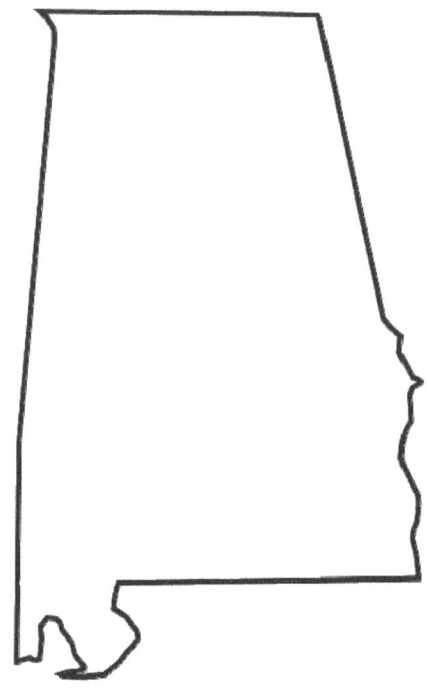

State bird_____

State capital_____

State motto_____

State nickname_____

State song_____

State tree_____

Alaska

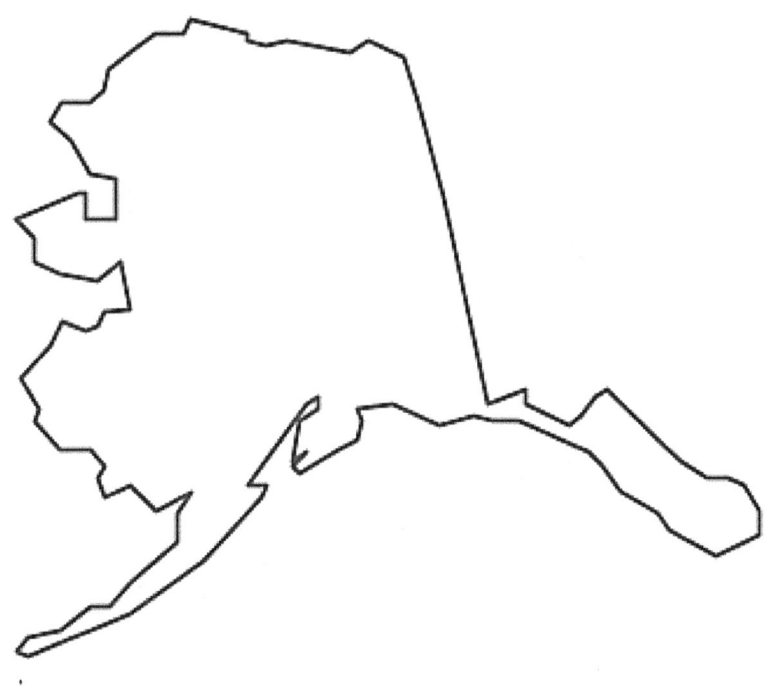

State bird_____

State capital_____

State motto_____

State nickname_____

State song_____

State tree_____

Arizona

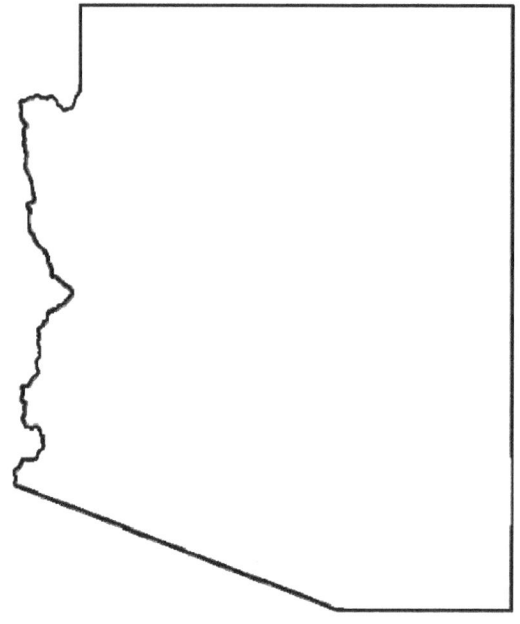

State bird_____

State capital_____

State motto_____

State nickname_____

State song_____

State tree_____

Arkansas

State bird _____

State capital _____

State motto _____

State nickname _____

State song _____

State tree _____

California

State bird_____

State capital_____

State motto_____

State nickname_____

State song_____

State tree_____

Colorado

State bird_____

State capital_____

State motto_____

State nickname_____

State song_____

State tree_____

Connecticut

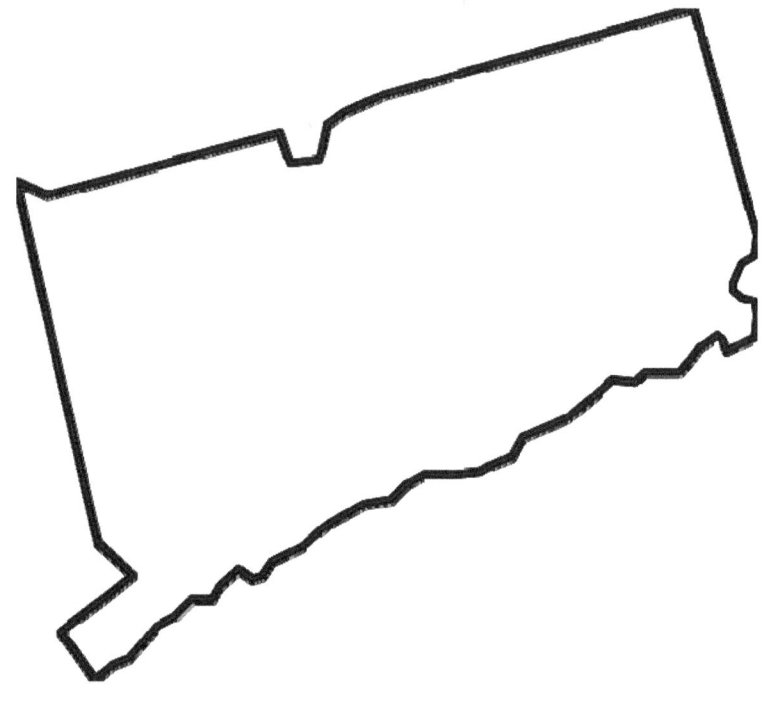

State bird_____

State capital_____

State motto_____

State nickname_____

State song_____

State tree_____

Delaware

State bird_____

State capital_____

State motto_____

State nickname_____

State song_____

State tree_____

Florida

State bird _____

State capital _____

State motto _____

State nickname _____

State song _____

State tree _____

Georgia

State bird_____

State capital_____

State motto_____

State nickname_____

State song_____

State tree_____

Hawaii

State bird _____

State capital _____

State motto _____

State nickname _____

State song _____

State tree _____

Idaho

State bird_____

State capital_____

State motto_____

State nickname_____

State song_____

State tree_____

Illinois

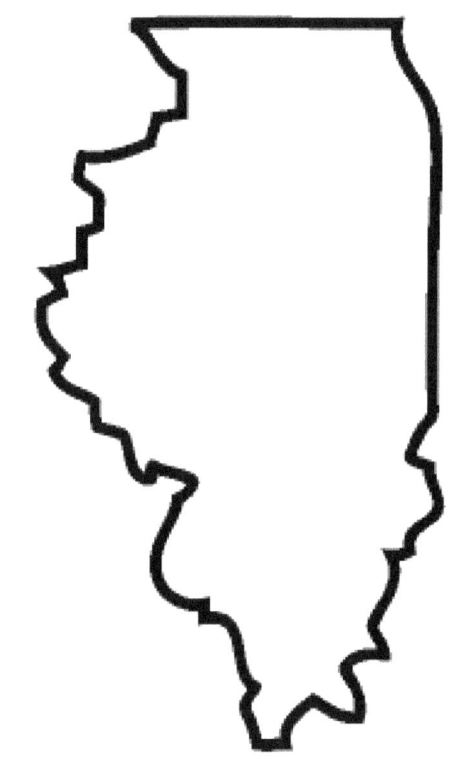

State bird_____

State capital_____

State motto_____

State nickname_____

State song_____

State tree_____

Indiana

State bird_____

State capital_____

State motto_____

State nickname_____

State song_____

State tree_____

Iowa

State bird_____

State capital_____

State motto_____

State nickname_____

State song_____

State tree_____

Kansas

State bird_____

State capital_____

State motto_____

State nickname_____

State song_____

State tree_____

Kentucky

State bird_____

State capital_____

State motto_____

State nickname_____

State song_____

State tree_____

Louisiana

State bird_____

State capital_____

State motto_____

State nickname_____

State song_____

State tree_____

Maine

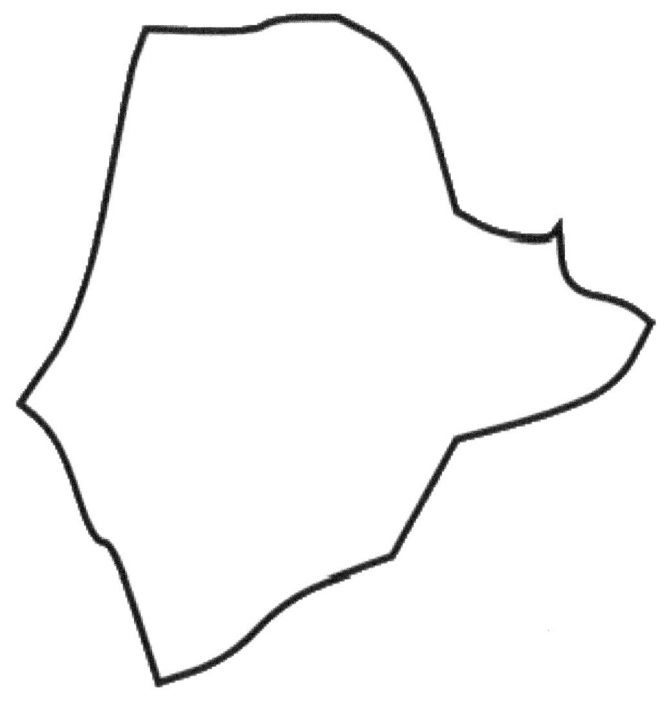

State bird_____

State capital_____

State motto_____

State nickname_____

State song_____

State tree_____

Maryland

State bird _____

State capital _____

State motto _____

State nickname _____

State song _____

State tree _____

Massachusetts

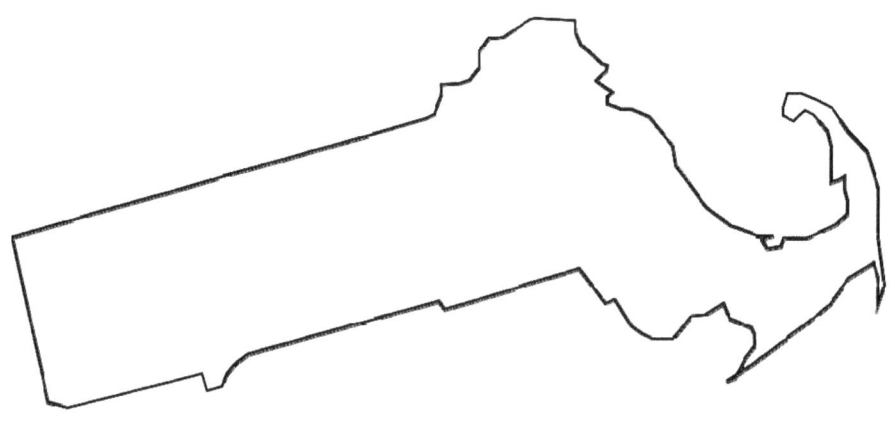

State bird_____

State capital_____

State motto_____

State nickname_____

State song_____

State tree_____

Michigan

State bird_____

State capital_____

State motto_____

State nickname_____

State song_____

State tree_____

Minnesota

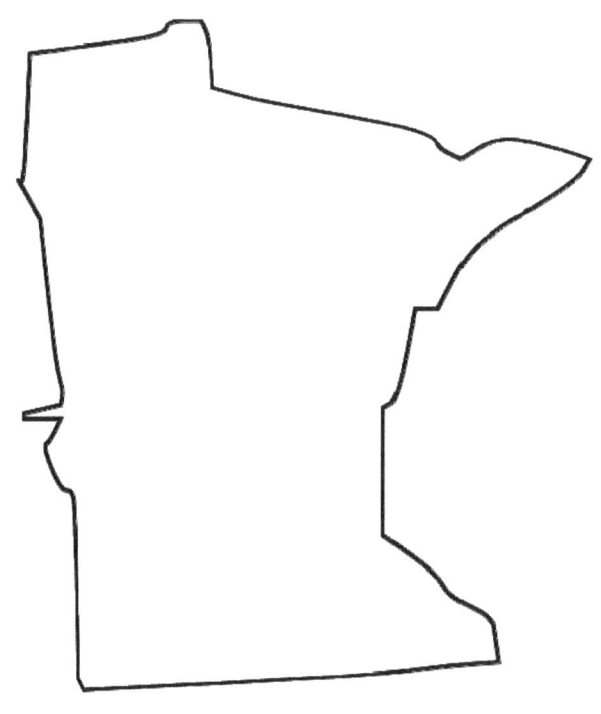

State bird_____

State capital_____

State motto_____

State nickname_____

State song_____

State tree_____

Mississippi

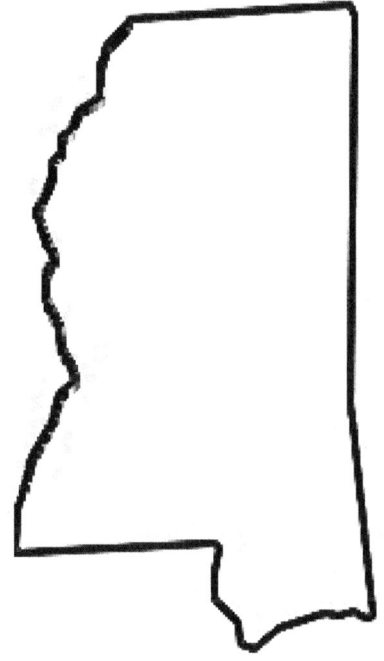

State bird_____

State capital_____

State motto_____

State nickname_____

State song_____

State tree_____

Missouri

State bird_____

State capital_____

State motto_____

State nickname_____

State song_____

State tree_____

Montana

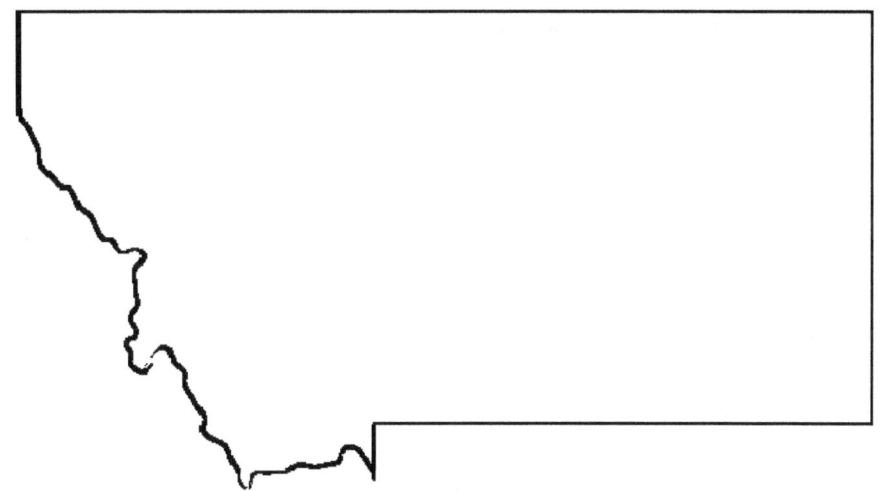

State bird_____

State capital_____

State motto_____

State nickname_____

State song_____

State tree_____

Nebraska

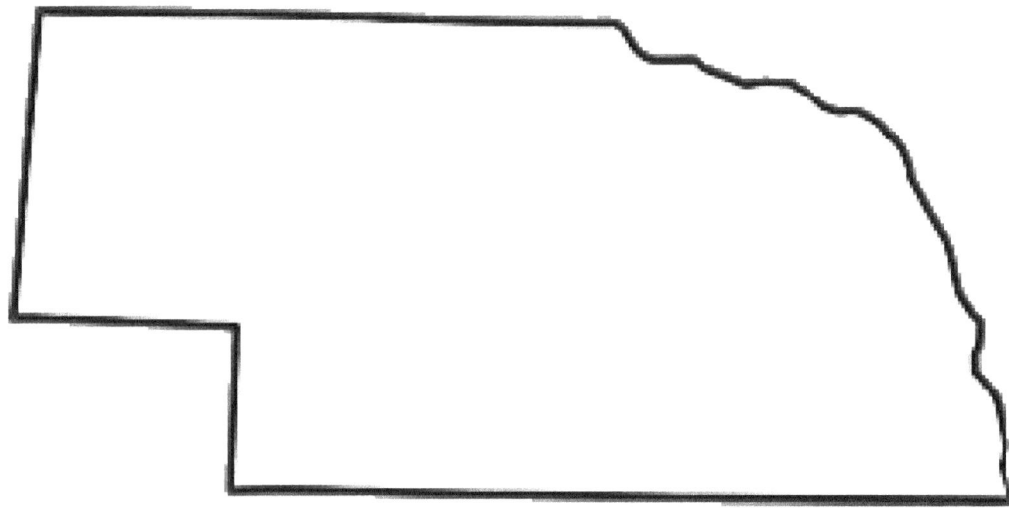

State bird_____

State capital_____

State motto_____

State nickname_____

State song_____

State tree_____

Nevada

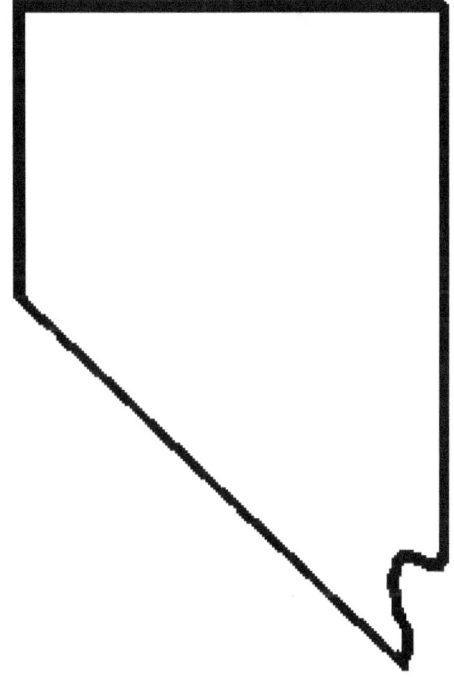

State bird_____

State capital_____

State motto_____

State nickname_____

State song_____

State tree_____

New Hampshire

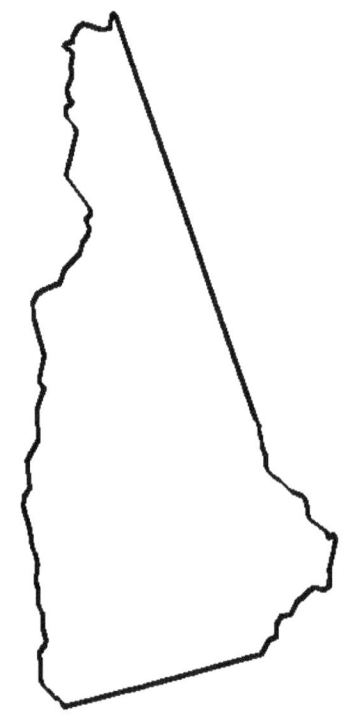

State bird_____

State capital_____

State motto_____

State nickname_____

State song_____

State tree_____

New Jersey

State bird_____

State capital_____

State motto_____

State nickname_____

State song_____

State tree_____

New Mexico

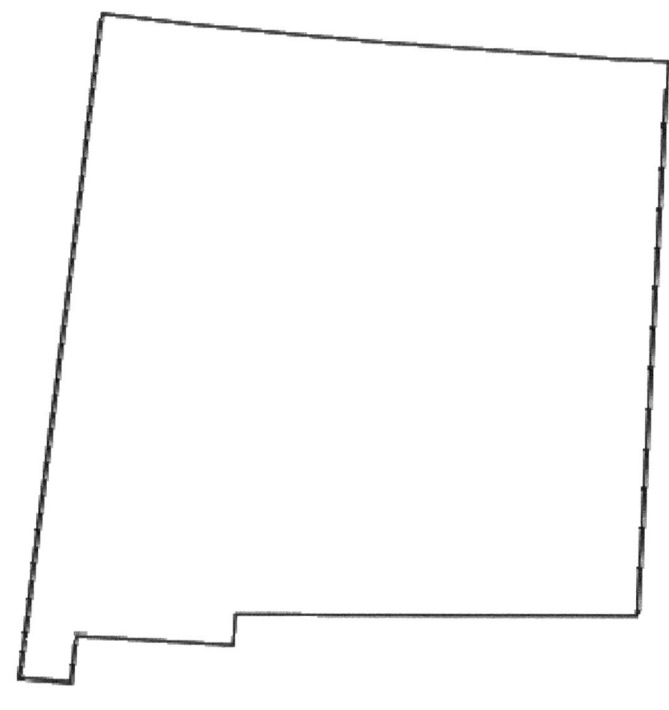

State bird_____

State capital_____

State motto_____

State nickname_____

State song_____

State tree_____

New York

State bird_____

State capital_____

State motto_____

State nickname_____

State song_____

State tree_____

North Carolina

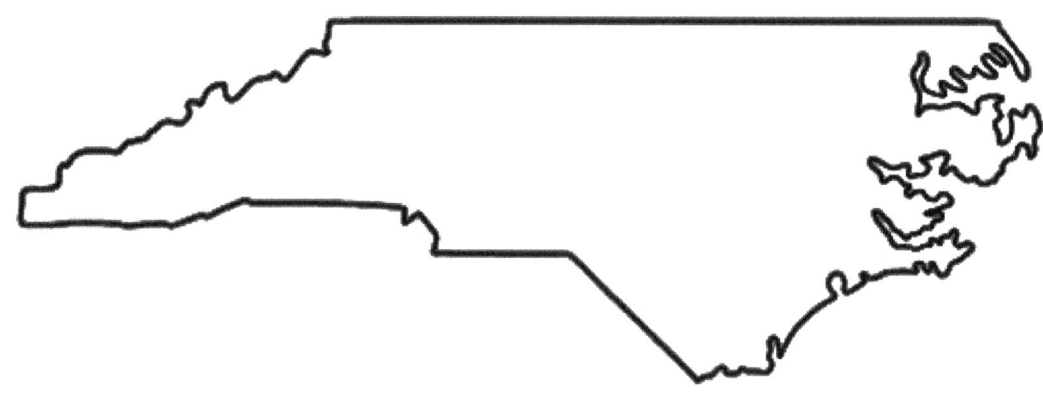

State bird_____

State capital_____

State motto_____

State nickname_____

State song_____

State tree_____

North Dakota

State bird_____

State capital_____

State motto_____

State nickname_____

State song_____

State tree_____

Ohio

State bird_____

State capital_____

State motto_____

State nickname_____

State song_____

State tree_____

Oklahoma

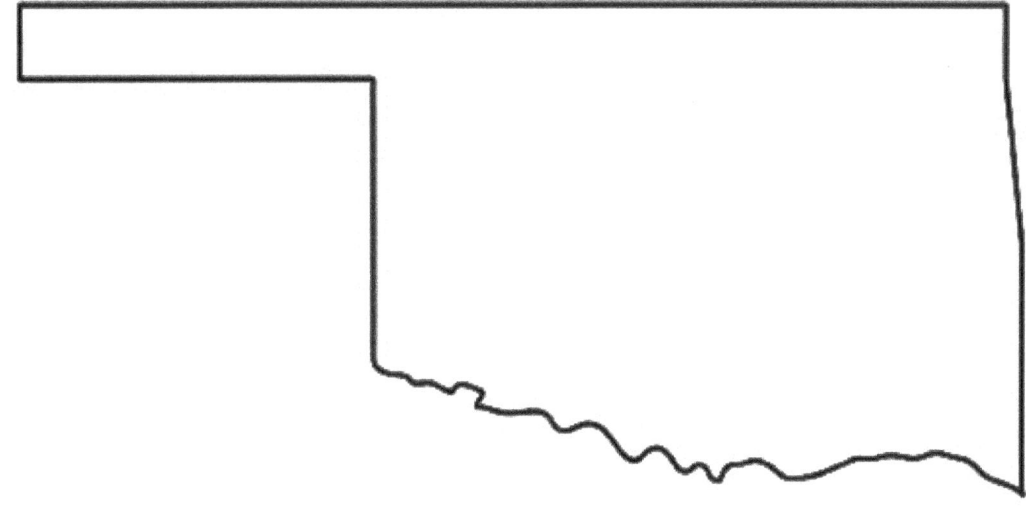

State bird_____

State capital_____

State motto_____

State nickname_____

State song_____

State tree_____

Oregon

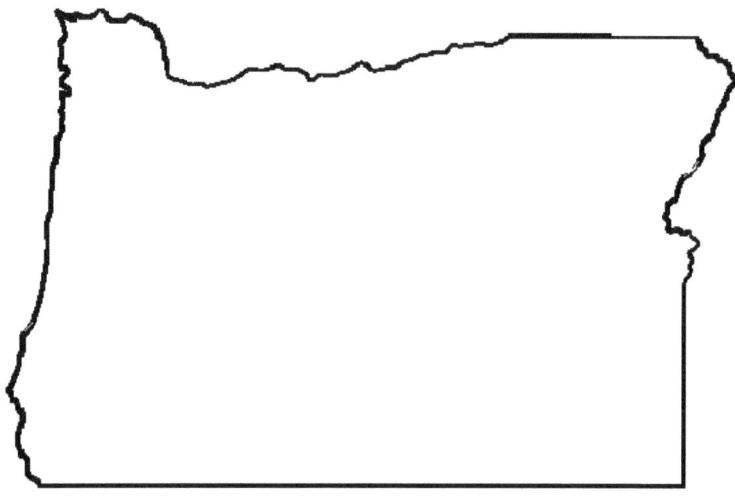

State bird_____

State capital_____

State motto_____

State nickname_____

State song_____

State tree_____

Pennsylvania

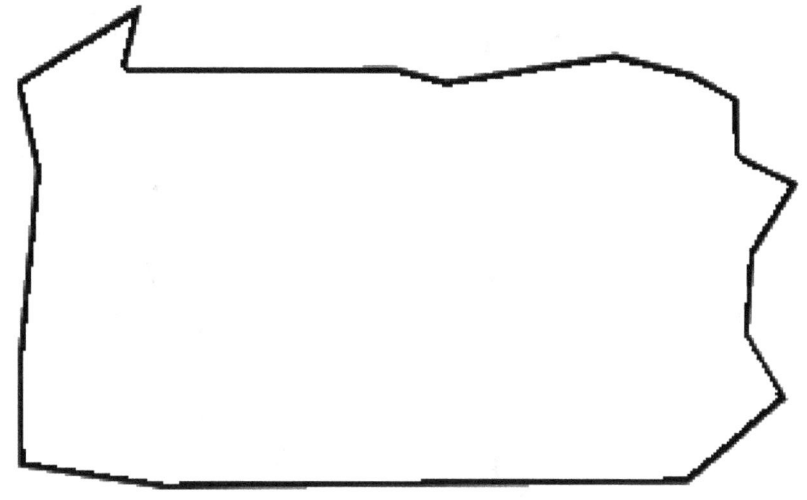

State bird_____

State capital_____

State motto_____

State nickname_____

State song_____

State tree_____

Rhode Island

State bird_____

State capital_____

State motto_____

State nickname_____

State song_____

State tree_____

South Carolina

State bird_____

State capital_____

State motto_____

State nickname_____

State song_____

State tree_____

South Dakota

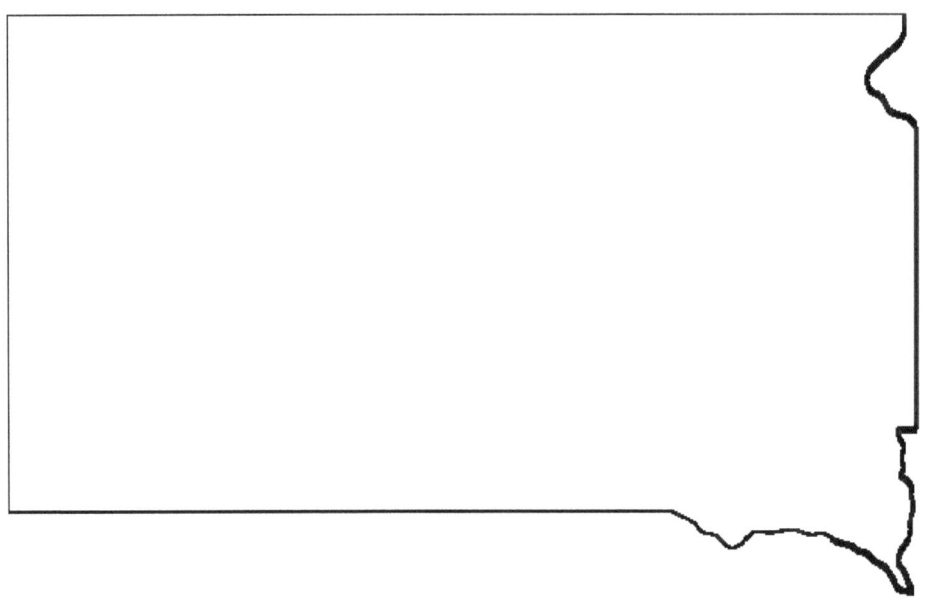

State bird_____

State capital_____

State motto_____

State nickname_____

State song_____

State tree_____

Tennessee

State bird_____

State capital_____

State motto_____

State nickname_____

State song_____

State tree_____

Texas

State bird_____

State capital_____

State motto_____

State nickname_____

State song_____

State tree_____

Utah

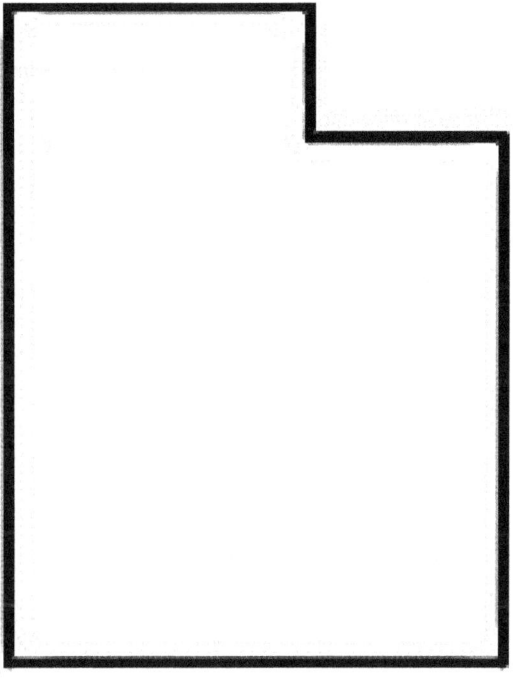

State bird_____

State capital_____

State motto_____

State nickname_____

State song_____

State tree_____

Vermont

State bird_____

State capital_____

State motto_____

State nickname_____

State song_____

State tree_____

Virginia

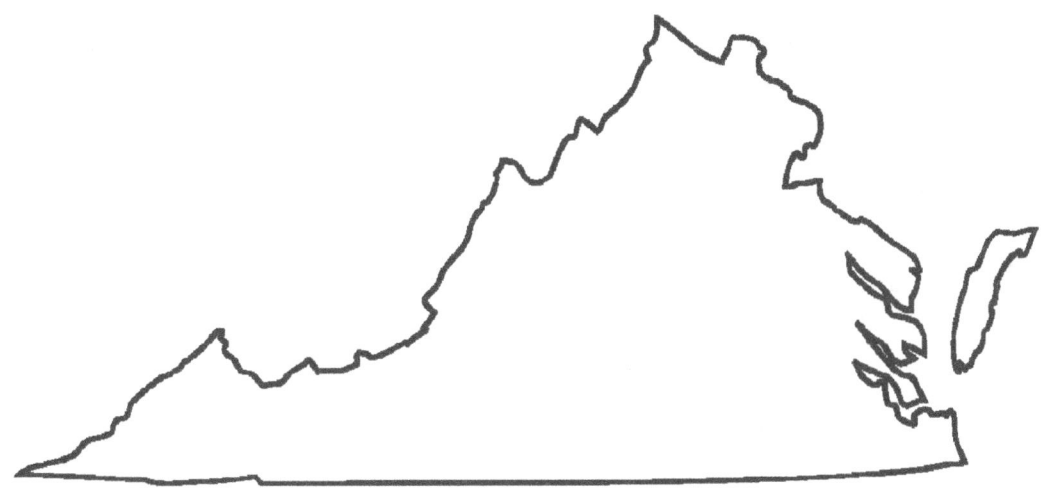

State bird_____

State capital_____

State motto_____

State nickname_____

State song_____

State tree_____

Washington

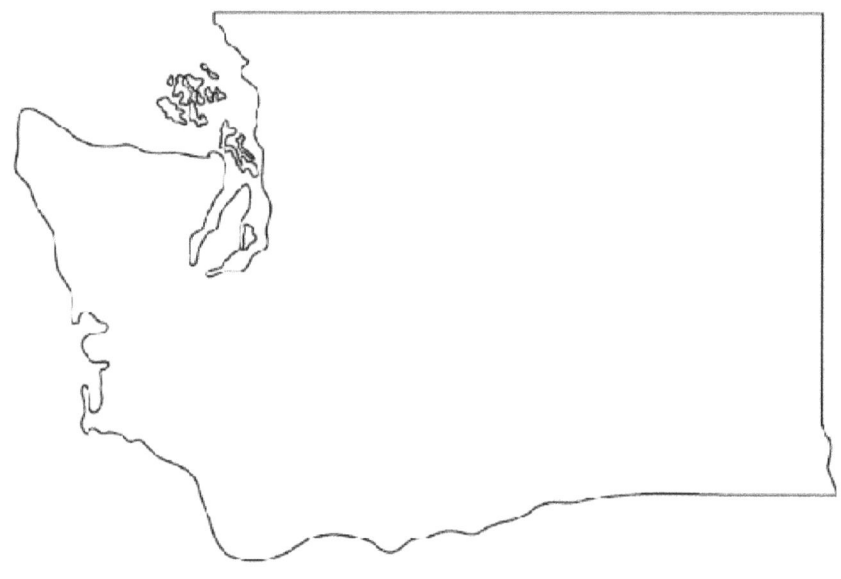

State bird_____

State capital_____

State motto_____

State nickname_____

State song_____

State tree_____

West Virginia

State bird_____

State capital_____

State motto_____

State nickname_____

State song_____

State tree_____

Wisconsin

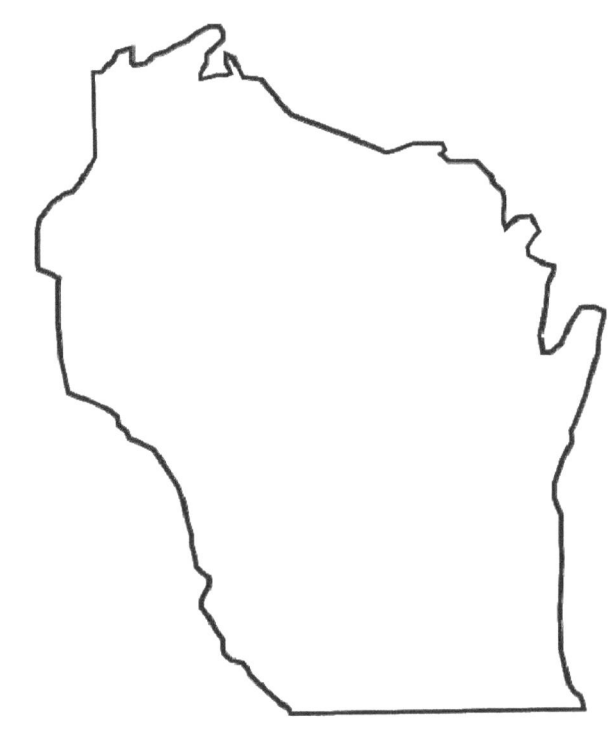

State bird_____

State capital_____

State motto_____

State nickname_____

State song_____

State tree_____

Wyoming

State bird_____

State capital_____

State motto_____

State nickname_____

State song_____

State tree_____

District of Columbia

Fun Facts

*Known as Washington, DC

*The United States capital

*Located on the Potomac River

*Borders Maryland and Virginia

*Location of the federal governments three branches:

    United States Capitol

    White House

    Supreme Court

*Not a part of any state

Continents and Oceans

Seven Continents:

Africa

Asia

Antarctica

Australia

Europe

North America

South America

Five Oceans:

Arctic Ocean

Atlantic Ocean

Indian Ocean

Pacific Ocean

*Southern Ocean

*(Also known as Antarctic Ocean)

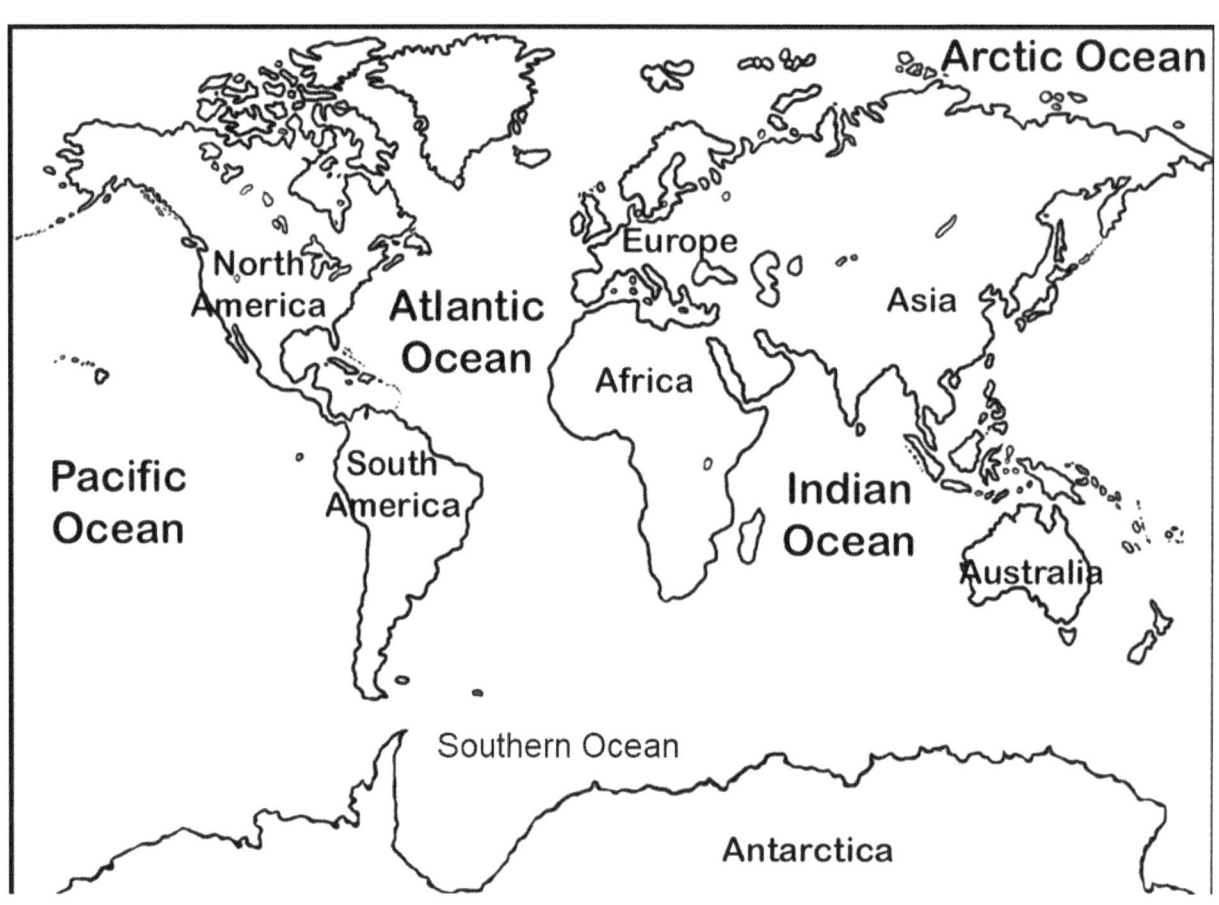

List the seven continents:

1. _____
2. _____
3. _____
4. _____
5. _____
6. _____
7. _____

List the five oceans:

1. _____
2. _____
3. _____
4. _____
5. _____
6. _____
7. _____

READING COMPREHENSION

Kindergarten and First Grade Common Sight Words

a	has	me
am	have	my
an	he	no
and	here	said
are	in	see
can	is	she
do	it	so
down	I	the
for	like	up
go	look	we

Alex

Alex likes to read books about animals. Every Saturday Alex big brother takes her to the Main Library. The library is a place with lots of books. There she gets to check out books to take home. At night, Alex reads a book before going to sleep.

Questions:
1. What does Alex like to do?
2. What does Alex like to read about?
3. Where does Alex go every Saturday?
4. Who took Alex to the library?
5. When does Alex read her book?

Baking Cookies

Cheryl wanted to bake some cookies for her friends. She knew everyone loved chocolate chip cookies. But when Cheryl looked in the cabinets there were not enough ingredients. This is what she needed to bake the cookies:

1. Flour
2. Butter
3. Light brown sugar
4. Sugar
5. Eggs
6. Vanilla favoring
7. Chocolate chip pieces

Questions:

1. What did Cheryl want to bake?

2. Whom was she baking the cookies for?

3. What kind of cookies did her friends like?

4. What are the ingredients for the cookies?

Michael and Meka

Michael rides the school bus every morning to school. He sits next to his friend Meka. They live in the same neighborhood. Meka likes bananas. Sometimes Michael brings her a banana for their morning snack. For their afternoon snack, Michael and Meka share a bag of popcorn. It is his favorite food. He wishes that he could eat it every day. After school, the friends will eat an apple while waiting for the school bus.

Questions:

1. Meka and Michael are_____.
2. They ride the _____.
3. Meka likes _____.
4. Michael's favorite food is_____.
5. The banana is for their _____.
6. Popcorn is for their _____.
7. After school they eat_____.

At The Zoo

First I saw the white bear, then I saw the black;

Then I saw the camel with a hump upon his back;

Then I saw the grey wolf, with mutton in his maw;

Then I saw the wombat waddle in the straw;

Then I saw the elephant a-waving of his trunk;

Then I saw the monkeys-mercy, how unpleasantly

they-smelt!

Questions:

1. What is the poem about?
2. What was the first animal?
3. How many bears are there?
4. What does the camel have on his back?
5. What was the elephant doing?
6. What is the last animal in the poem?
7. How did the monkey smell?

* Poem written by William Makepeace Thackeray

A Day With Grandma

Thomas and Jessica always love going to the park with Grandma Jessie. There are many fun things for them to see and do especially riding the merry-go-round. The merry-go-round has seats in the shape of teacups and animals that move up and down. Each seat and animal is a different color. Riding the pink horse gives Jessica the most joy. Thomas thinks that the lion is the best seat. He pretends to roar like a lion while riding it. As Grandma Jessie sits in the purple teacup, she pretends that she is drinking a cup of tea and eating cookies.

Everyone likes the different animals living in the park. Each animal has their own sleeping area. The monkey has a tree to climb. There is a pond with different types of fish. Watching the geese cross the sidewalks is always exciting. The biggest one in the group stands in the middle of the sidewalk until all the others have crossed it.

The best part of going to the park with Grandma Jessie is having ice cream. Thomas likes vanilla with sprinkles in a cup. Jessica chooses strawberry in a waffle cone. Banana splits are grandma's favorite especially with cherries on top. There is nothing greater than spending the day with Grandma Jessie.

Questions:
1. Name the people in the story.
2. Where does Grandma Jessie take Jessica and Thomas?
3. What is everyone's favorite thing to do at the park?
4. Describe the merry-go-round.
5. What does grandma pretend to do while she is riding in the teacup?
6. Name the animals in the park.
7. What animal does everyone think is the most exciting?
8. What is the best part of going to the park?
9. What kind of ice cream does everyone like?

Mother's Day

In a few weeks it would be Mother's Day. The three sisters did not know what to get for their mother. They decided to add up their savings to see how much money they each had. Mary counted seven dollars in her jewelry box. Maggie's shoebox contained five dollars. Inside May's sock was three dollars. What could they buy their mother?

The three girls thought for a very long time. Did they have enough for a special gift? Mary the oldest of the three, remembered what their mother taught them. The best gifts come from the heart. Each of the sisters has a special talent. Mary is an artist. Maggie, the middle girl enjoys writing. May, the youngest daughter, likes to build things out of wood.

The sisters decided to make a special gift for Mother's Day. Mary painted a picture of the girls standing in a flower garden. Maggie wrote a poem called "Mother's Garden". May built a frame to hold the picture and poem. When the gift was finished, the three knew that they had made the best gift in the world…one that came from their heart.

Questions:

1. What is the name of the story?

2. How many sisters are there?

3. How much money does each of the sisters have?

4. What is the total amount of money the sisters have together?

5. Whom did they want to make a gift for?

6. Where does the best gift come from?

7. What is a talent?

8. Name each of the sister's talent.

9. How did they use their talents?

Literature: Past and Present

My Shadow

I have a little shadow that goes in and out with me,

And what can be the use of him is more than I can see.

He is very, very like me from the heels up to the head;

And I see him jump before me, when I jump into my bed.

The funniest thing about him is the way he likes to grow-

Not at all like proper children, which is always very slow;

For he sometimes shoots up taller like an india-rubber ball,

And he sometimes gets so little that there's none of him at all.

He hasn't got a notion of how children ought to play,

And can only make a fool of me in every sort of way.

He stays so close beside me, he's a coward you can see;

I'd think shame to stick to nursie as that shadow sticks to me!

One morning, very early, before the sun was up,

I rose and found the shining dew on every buttercup;

But my lazy little shadow, like an arrant sleepy-head,

Had stayed at home behind me and was fast asleep in bed.

by Robert Louis Stevenson

Dreams

What dreams we have and how they fly

Like rosy clouds across the sky;

Of wealth, of fame, of sure success,

Of love that comes to cheer and bless;

And how they wither, how they fade,

The waning wealth, the jilting jade -

The fame that for a moment gleams,

Then flies forever, -dreams, ah -dreams!

O burning doubt and long regret

O tears with which our eyes are wet,

Heart-throbs, heart-aches, the glut of pain,

The somber cloud, the bitter rain,

You were not of those dreams - ah! well,

Your full fruition who can tell?

Wealth, fame, and love, ah! love that beams

Upon our souls, all dreams - ah! dreams.

by Paul Laurence Dunbar

Trees

I think that I shall never see

A poem lovely as a tree.

A tree whose hungry mouth is press

Against the sweet earth's flowing breast;

A tree that looks at God all day,

And lifts her leafy arms to pray;

A tree that may in summer wear

A nest of robins in her hair;

Upon whose bosom snow has lain;

Who intimately lives with rain.

Poems are made by fools like me,

But only God can make a tree.

By Joyce Kilmer

A-Tisket, a-Tasket

A-tisket a-tasket
A green and yellow basket
I wrote a letter to my love
And on the way I dropped it

I dropped it, I dropped it
Yes, on the way I dropped it
A little girlie picked it up
And took it to the market
She was truckin' on down the avenue
Without a single thing to do
She was peck, peck, peckin' all around
When she spied it on the ground

A-tisket a-tasket
She took my yellow basket
And if she doesn't bring it back
I think that I shall die

A-tisket a-tasket
A green and yellow basket
I wrote a letter to my love
And on the way I dropped it

I dropped it, I dropped it
Yes, on the way I dropped it
A little girlie picked it up
And took it to the market

(Was it red?) No, no, no, no
(Was it brown?) No, no, no, no
(Was it blue?) No, no, no, no
Just a little yellow basket

Written during the late nineteen century-1879

***

Good Morning Song

Good morning, good morning, good morning to you
Good morning, good morning, good morning to you
Our day is beginning, there's so much to do
So, good morning, good morning, good morning to you

Authors and copyright status unknown

Twinkle, Twinkle Little Star

Twinkle, twinkle, little star,
How I wonder what you are.
Up above the world so high,
Like a diamond in the sky.
Twinkle, twinkle, little star,
How I wonder what you are!

When the blazing sun is gone,
When he nothing shines upon,
Then you show your little light,
Twinkle, twinkle, all the night.
Twinkle, twinkle, little star,
How I wonder what you are!

Then the traveler in the dark
Thanks you for your tiny spark;
He could not see which way to go,
If you did not twinkle so.
Twinkle, twinkle, little star,
How I wonder what you are!

In the dark blue sky you keep,
While you thro' my window peep,
And you never shut your eye,
Till the sun is in the sky,
Twinkle, twinkle, little star,
How I wonder what you are!

Jane Taylor (1806)

***

Baa, Baa, Black Sheep

Baa, baa, black sheep,
Have you any wool?
Yes sir, yes sir,
Three bags full.

One for the master,
One for the dame,
And one for the little boy
Who lives down the lane.

Baa, baa, black sheep,
Have you any wool?
Yes sir, yes sir,
Three bags full.

One to mend the jerseys
one to mend the socks
and one to mend the holes in
the little girls' frocks.

Baa, baa, black sheep,
Have you any wool?
Yes sir, yes sir,
Three bags full.

Authors and copyright status unknown

Loop de Loop (or Looby Loo)

Here we go loop de loop
Here we go loop de lie
Here we go loop de loop
All on a Saturday night

You put your right hand in
You take your right hand out
You give your hand a shake,
shake, shake
And turn yourself about

Here we go loop de loop
Here we go loop de lie
Here we go loop de loop
All on a Saturday night

You put your left foot in
You take your left foot out
You give your foot a shake,
shake, shake
And turn yourself about

Here we go loop de loop
Here we go loop de lie
Here we go loop de loop
All on a Saturday night

You put your right hip in
You take your right hip out
You give your right hip a
shake, shake, shake
And turn yourself about

Here we go loop de loop
Here we go loop de lie
Here we go loop de loop
All on a Saturday night

You put your whole self in
You take your whole self out
You give yourself a shake,
shake, shake
And turn yourself about

Written and Copyright Dates Unknown

***

It's Raining, It's Pouring

It's raining, it's pouring;
The old man is snoring.
He went to bed and he
Bumped his head
And he couldn't get up in the morning.

Written and Copyright Dates Unknown

Thumbelina

A long time ago and far, far away an old woman was sitting in her rocking chair thinking how happy she would be if she had a child. Then, she heard a knock at the door and opened it. A lady was standing there and she said, "If you let me in, I will grant you a wish." The old woman let the woman in firstly because she felt pity, secondly because she knew what she'd wish for...a child. After she washed the lady up and fed her, she saw that she was really beautiful.

The lady slept soundly all night long and then right before she left, she said, "Now, about your wish. What do you want?"

The lady thought about most people's wishes to be richest in the world, most powerful person, the smartest, and the prettiest. But the old woman wished for something the lady could not believe. She said, "I would like a child."

"What did you say?" she asked because she was astonished at what the old lady asked for. The old lady repeated what she said. "I would like a child."

The lady then placed a tiny seed in the old woman's hand and gave her instructions. " Plant this seed, water it carefully, watch over it, and give it your love. If you do all those things, then you will have a child."

So the old woman did all of those things the lady had told her to. In a week, there was a beautiful yellow flower in place of the seed. The next day, the flower bloomed. Inside the flower was a beautiful little girl who was the size of the woman's thumb so she a called her Thumbellina. She made her a little dress out of golden threads. Thumbellina slept in a walnut shell and brought the old woman joy and happiness.

But, one day when Thumbellina went down for her nap, a frog hopped through the open window and said, "You will be a perfect bride for my son," and she took Thumbellina to a lily pad and hopped off to find her son.

Thumbellina cried and some little guppies heard her and chewed the roots off the lily pad to help her escape. Thumbellina's lily pad floated away. A few hours later, she finally stopped floating. During the summer, she ate berries and drank the dew off the leaves. But then winter came and she needed shelter. A kindly mouse let her stay with it, but it said, "You'll have to marry my friend, Mole, because I cannot keep you for another winter."

The next day she went to see Mole. In one of tunnels, she found a sick bird and said, "Poor thing, I will bury it." Then she found out that it was still alive and she cared for it until was ready to fly. It flew off. That fall she nearly had to marry Mole. But then she heard a familiar tweet and an idea popped up in the bird's head.

"You can come down to the warm country," said the bird, so Thumbellina hopped on the bird's back and flew to the warm country. The people there who were like her renamed her Erin. She married a prince and she lived happily ever after.

The End

THE TALE OF PETER RABBIT

BY
BEATRIX POTTER

NEW YORK
FREDERICK WARNE & CO., INC.

*Copyright in all countries
signatory to the Berne Convention*

[All rights reserved]

Ord Edn 7232 0592 2
Lib Edn 7232 0615 5

The Original
Peter Rabbit Books
By BEATRIX POTTER

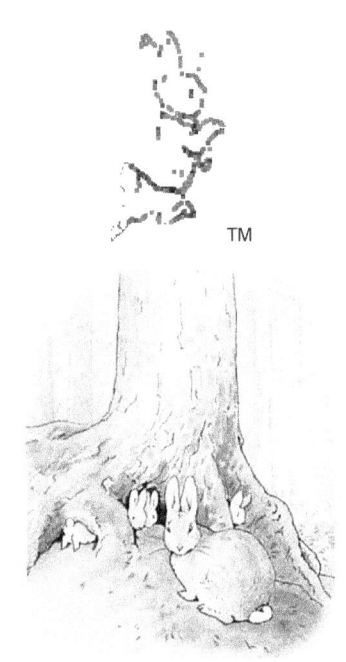

Once upon a time there were four little Rabbits, and their names were—

Flopsy,
Mopsy,
Cotton-tail,
and Peter.

They lived with their Mother in a sand-bank, underneath the root of a very big fir-tree.

'Now, my dears,' said old Mrs. Rabbit one morning, 'you may go into the fields or down the lane, but don't go into Mr. McGregor's garden: your Father had an accident there; he was put in a pie by Mrs. McGregor.'

'NOW run along, and don't get into mischief. I am going out.'

THEN old Mrs. Rabbit took a basket and her umbrella, and went through the wood to the baker's. She bought a loaf of brown bread and five currant buns.

FLOPSY, Mopsy, and Cotton-tail, who were good little bunnies, went down the lane to gather blackberries:

BUT Peter, who was very naughty, ran straight away to Mr. McGregor's garden, and squeezed under the gate!

FIRST he ate some lettuces and some French beans; and then he ate some radishes;

AND then, feeling rather sick, he went to look for some parsley.

But round the end of a cucumber frame, whom should he meet but Mr. McGregor!

Mr. McGregor was on his hands and knees planting out young cabbages, but he jumped up and ran after Peter, waving a rake and calling out, 'Stop thief!'

PETER was most dreadfully frightened; he rushed all over the garden, for he had forgotten the way back to the gate.

He lost one of his shoes among the cabbages, and the other shoe amongst the potatoes.

AFTER losing them, he ran on four legs and went faster, so that I think he might have got away altogether if he had not unfortunately run into a gooseberry net, and got caught by the large buttons on his jacket. It was a blue jacket with brass buttons, quite new.

PETER gave himself up for lost, and cried big tears; but his sobs were overheard by some friendly sparrows, who flew to him in great excitement, and implored him to exert himself.

MR. McGREGOR came up with a sieve, which he intended to pop upon the top of Peter; but Peter wriggled out just in time, leaving his jacket behind him.

AND rushed into the tool-shed, and jumped into a can. It would have been a beautiful thing to hide in, if it had not had so much water in it.

MR. McGREGOR was quite sure that Peter was somewhere in the tool-shed, perhaps hidden underneath a flower-pot. He began to turn them over carefully, looking under each.

Presently Peter sneezed—'Kertyschoo!' Mr. McGregor was after him in no time.

AND tried to put his foot upon Peter, who jumped out of a window, upsetting three plants. The window was too small for Mr. McGregor, and he was tired of running after Peter. He went back to his work.

PETER sat down to rest; he was out of breath and trembling with fright, and he had not the least idea which way to go. Also he was very damp with sitting in that can.

After a time he began to wander about, going lippity—lippity—not very fast, and looking all round.

An old mouse was running in and out over the stone door-step, carrying peas and beans to her family in the wood. Peter asked her the way to the gate, but she had such a large pea in her mouth that she could not answer. She shook her head at him. Peter began to cry.

THEN he tried to find his way straight across the garden, but he became more and more puzzled. Presently, he came to a pond where Mr. McGregor filled his water-cans. A white cat was staring at some gold-fish, she sat very, very still, but now and then the tip of her tail twitched as if it were alive. Peter thought it best to go away without speaking to her; he had heard about cats from his cousin, little Benjamin Bunny.

HE went back towards the tool-shed, but suddenly, quite close to him, he heard the noise of a hoe—scr-r-ritch, scratch, scratch, scritch. Peter scuttered underneath the bushes. But presently, as nothing happened, he came out, and climbed upon a wheelbarrow and peeped over. The first thing he saw was Mr. McGregor hoeing onions. His back was turned towards Peter, and beyond him was the gate!

PETER got down very quietly off the wheelbarrow, and started running as fast as he could go, along a straight walk behind some black-currant bushes.

Mr. McGregor caught sight of him at the corner, but Peter did not care. He slipped underneath the gate, and was safe at last in the wood outside the garden.

MR. McGREGOR hung up the little jacket and the shoes for a scare-crow to frighten the blackbirds.

PETER never stopped running or looked behind him till he got home to the big fir-tree.

He was so tired that he flopped down upon the nice soft sand on the floor of the rabbit-hole and shut his eyes. His mother was busy cooking; she wondered what he had done with his clothes. It was the second little jacket and pair of shoes that Peter had lost in a fortnight!

I AM sorry to say that Peter was not very well during the evening.

His mother put him to bed, and made some camomile tea; and she gave a dose of it to Peter!

'One table-spoonful to be taken at bed-time.'

BUT Flopsy, Mopsy, and Cotton-tail had bread and milk and blackberries for supper.

THE END

This work is in the **public domain** in the **United States** because it was published before January 1, 1923.

The author died in 1943, so this work is also in the **public domain** in countries and areas where the copyright term is the author's **life plus 70 years or less**. This work may also be in the **public domain** in countries and areas with longer native copyright terms that apply the **rule of the shorter term** to foreign works.

The Princess And The Pea
Written By
Hans Christian Anderson

ONCE upon a time there was a prince who wanted to marry a princess; but she would have to be a real princess. He travelled all over the world to find one, but nowhere could he get what he wanted. There were princesses enough, but it was difficult to find out whether they were real ones. There was always something about them that was not as it should be. So he came home again and was sad, for he would have liked very much to have a real princess.

One evening a terrible storm came on; there was thunder and lightning, and the rain poured down in torrents. Suddenly a knocking was heard at the city gate, and the old king went to open it.

It was a princess standing out there in front of the gate. But, good gracious! what a sight the rain and the wind had made her look. The water ran down from her hair and clothes; it ran down into the toes of her shoes and out again at the heels. And yet she said that she was a real princess.

Well, we'll soon find that out, thought the old queen. But she said nothing, went into the bed-room, took all the bedding off the bedstead, and laid a pea on the bottom; then she took twenty mattresses and laid them on the pea, and then twenty eider-down beds on top of the mattresses.

On this the princess had to lie all night. In the morning she was asked how she had slept.

Oh, very badly! said she. I have scarcely closed my eyes all night. Heaven only knows what was in the bed, but I was lying on something hard, so that I am black and blue all over my body. Its horrible!

Now they knew that she was a real princess because she had felt the pea right through the twenty mattresses and the twenty eider-down beds.

Nobody but a real princess could be as sensitive as that.

So the prince took her for his wife, for now he knew that he had a real princess; and the pea was put in the museum, where it may still be seen, if no one has stolen it.

There, that is a true story.

FOUR SEASONS

Written by

Donna McMillan

Winter

Spring

Summer

or Fall

?

Which one is the best of all?

Snow and hats,

coats and boots,

long days,

short nights,

I am winter
That's right!

In the spring comes April showers,

kites, grass

and colorful flowers!

Summer is here.

Oh boy what fun!

Ice cream,

swimming,

and that very hot sun!

Pumpkins and trees,

fallen brown leaves,

circus, and clowns,
fall is in town!

Winter

Spring

Summer

or Fall

?

Which one is the best of all?

Words to know

am	in
and	is
boy	of
come	or
here	the

Just For Fun

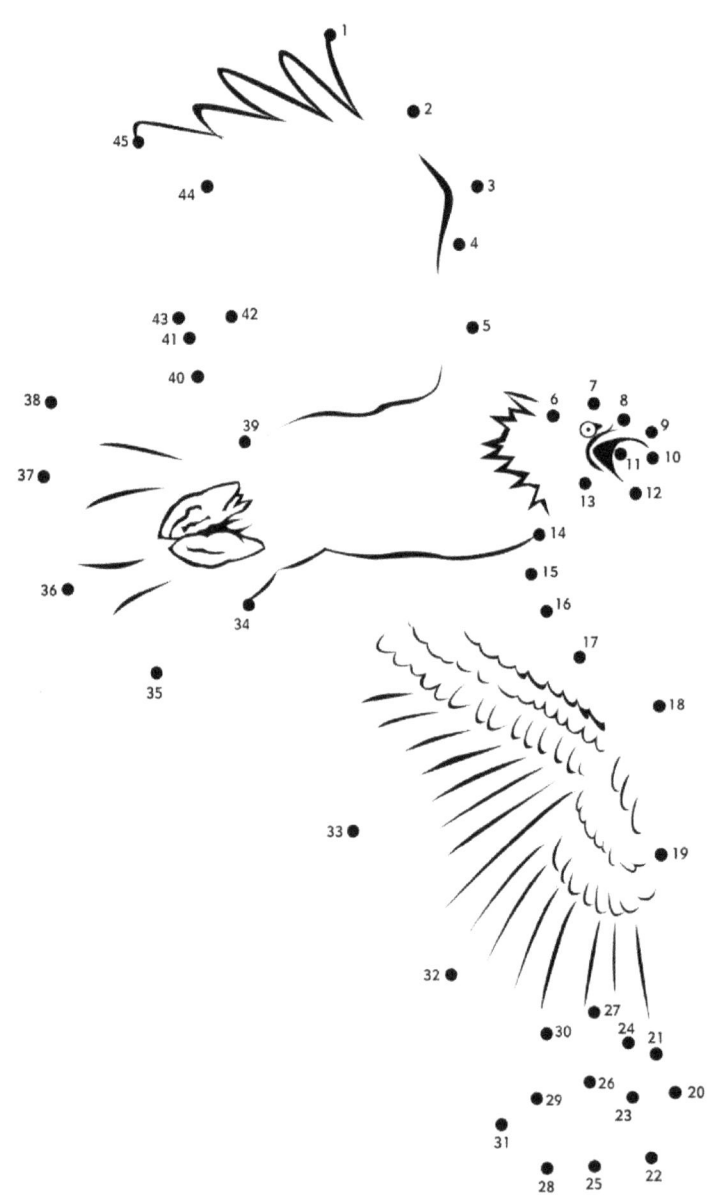

388

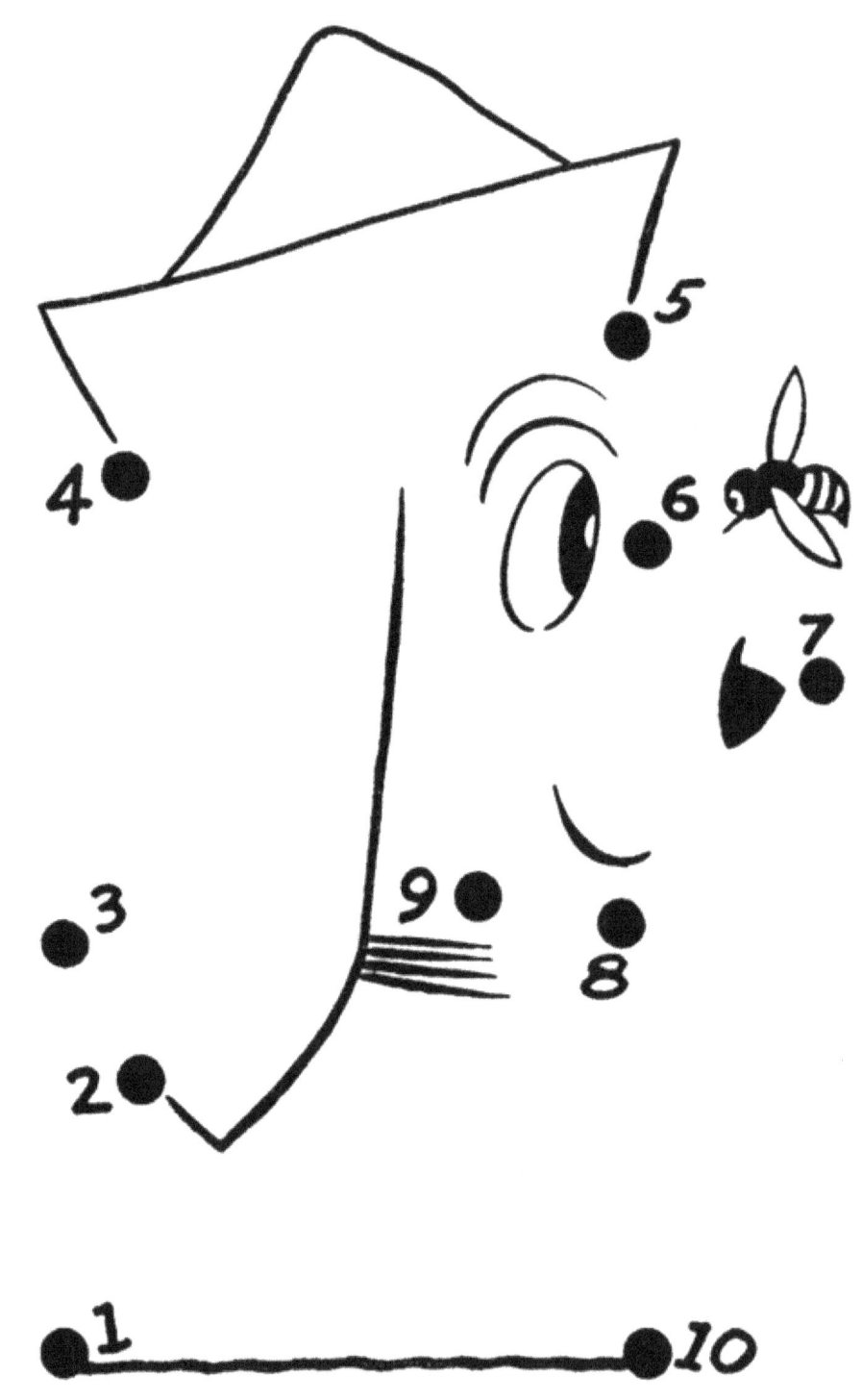

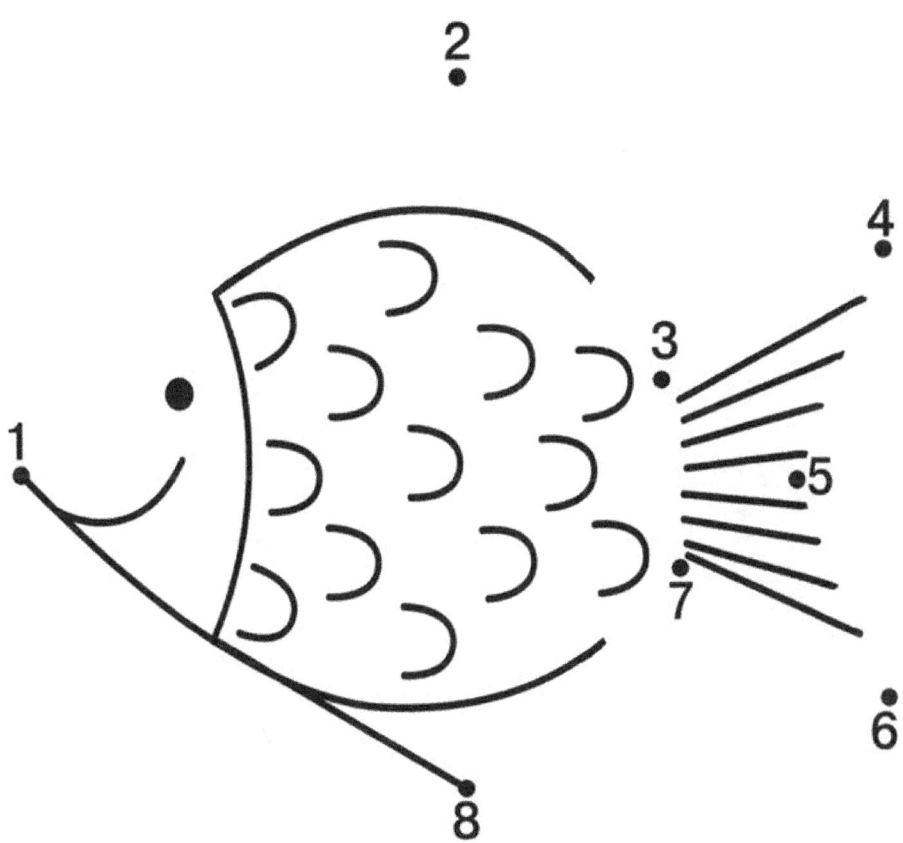

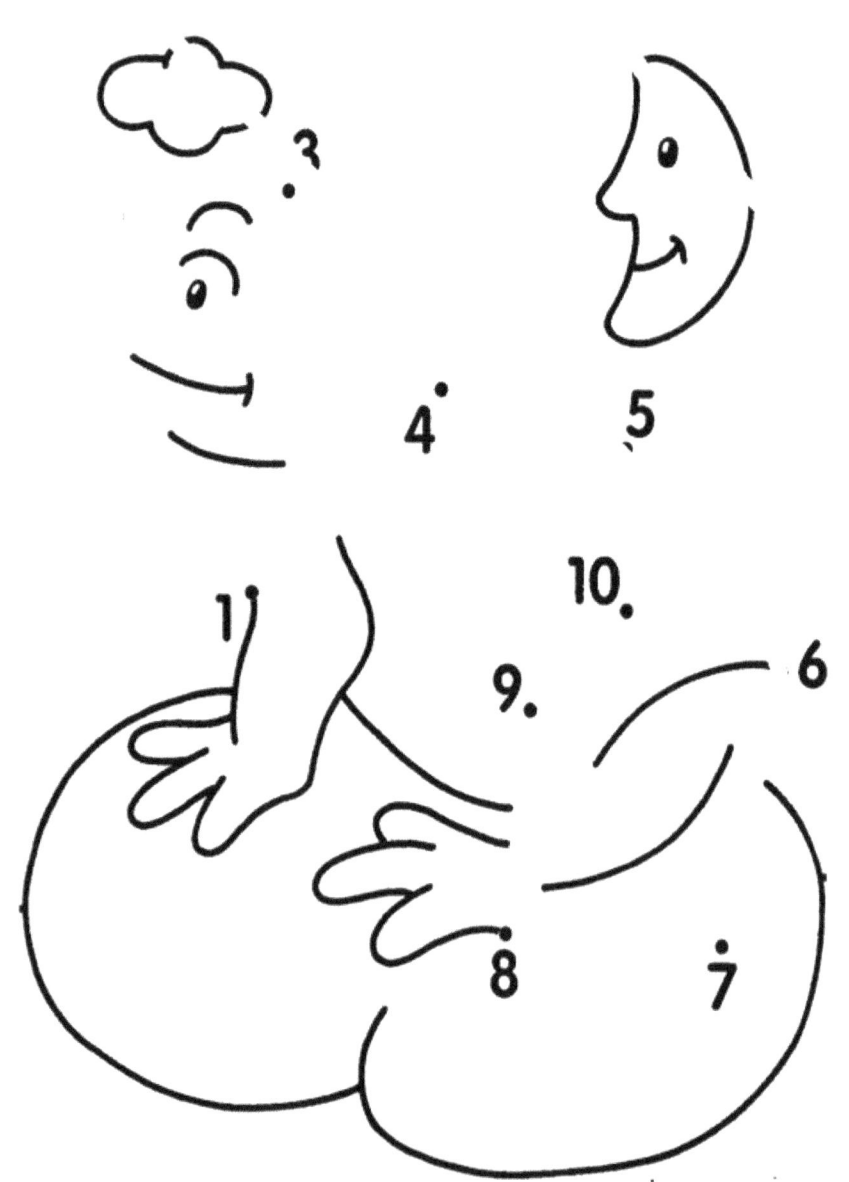

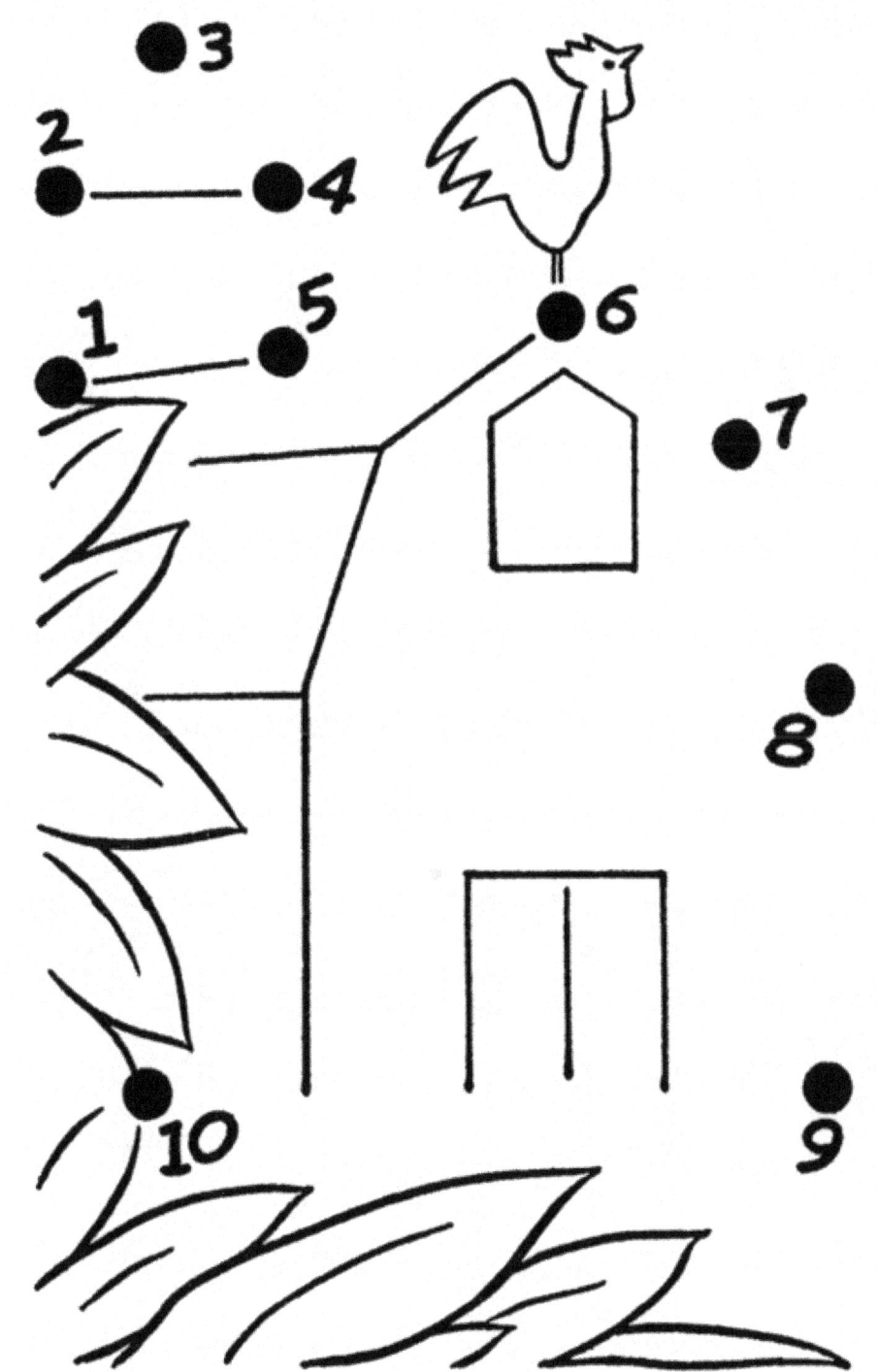

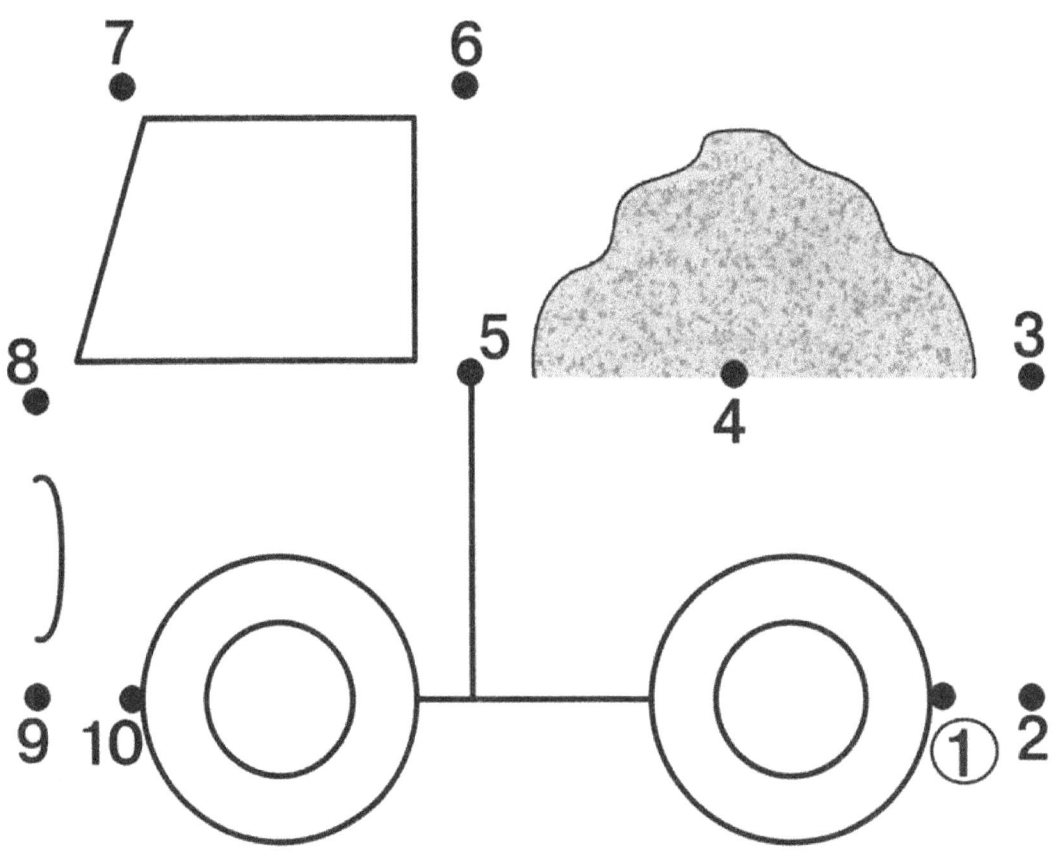

Birthday cake

Bb

This birthday cake is missing a candle! Kids draw a path from the cake to the candle by following the B's in the letter maze.

q	w	S	X	e	F	g	V	e	y	w	B	v	D	p
A	z	x	D	T	c	W	t	l	b	B	b	X	U	i
Q	a	W	q	a	Z	s	Y	N	B	z	G	o	m	J
E	s	B	b	B	b	B	Q	c	b	C	f	L	P	k
d	T	b	H	p	f	b	y	O	B	n	k	M	N	J
Z	r	B	A	S	r	B	l	h	b	b	B	b	V	u
d	G	B	m	P	C	b	B	j	L	o	j	B	K	p
h	F	b	Y	i	U	k	b	E	k	l	u	B	Z	l
O	l	B	H	p	o	q	b	b	B	B	b	B	N	r
C	j	b	B	b	R	l	f	N	K	z	R	m	U	c
l	e	n	c	B	z	N	Y	j	i	c	x	K	y	G
L	n	M	P	b	B	b	B	b	B	B	A	s	J	i
r	G	U	v	o	T	n	u	M	x	b	P	u	O	W
v	f	b	B	B	b	B	b	b	B	b	y	g	L	K
C	t	B	F	t	R	g	M	d	O	k	V	l	m	J

Acknowledgements

Public Domain Books, Illustrations, Poems, Stories, and Songs:

Clker, Creative Commons (CC BY-SA 3.0), Flicker, Pixabay, Wikipedia, and Wikisource.

Books, Illustrations, Poems, Stories, and Songs are in the public domain because:

1. The first publication occurred prior to January 1, 1923
2. 70 years has pass since the author's death

www.ingramcontent.com/pod-product-compliance
Lightning Source LLC
Chambersburg PA
CBHW081214170426
43198CB00017B/2609